Everyday Joy

*Or, How To Be Happier And Healthier,
and Party All The Time*

BY ZACHARY STOCKILL

Copyright © 2014 Zachary Stockill

http://www.zfstockill.com

Cover design by Alexander Joo Creative.

ALL RIGHTS RESERCED

This book contains material protected under International and Federal Copyright Laws and Treaties. Any unauthorized reprint or use of this material is prohibited. No part of this book may be reproduced or transmitted in any form or by any means, electronic or mechanical, including photocopying, recording, or by any information storage and retrieval system without express written permission from the author.

Requests for further information on usage of this document should be addressed to the author. Please send an email to zachary@zfstockill.com.

LEGAL NOTICE

The purchaser or reader of this publication assumes responsibility for the use of these materials and information. Adherence to all applicable laws and regulations—federal, state, local, and any other jurisdiction—is the sole responsibility of the purchaser or reader.

The author and publisher assume no responsibility or liability whatsoever on the behalf of any purchaser or reader of these materials.

Dedicated to the people of Medellín, Colombia

CONTENTS

	Acknowledgments	i
	Foreword	ii
	Introduction	11
1	Death	19
2	Funerals	27
3	Pain	33
4	Drugs	41
5	Loneliness	48
6	Love	55
7	Desire	63
8	Your Gift	69
9	Noble Sufferers	74
10	Complaining	79
11	The Joy of Others	87
12	Chasing Pleasure	93
13	Presence	101
	Conclusion	106
	Next Steps	112
	About the Author	114

ACKNOWLEDGMENTS

THANK-YOU to Zach Obront, Jane Bond, Alex Joo, Shama Adams, Cody McKibben, Ryan Stone, and everyone else who helped me with this book in its early stages. Your friendship and support was (and is) invaluable to me.

Thank-you to Mum and Dad for your unwavering love and encouragement.

Thanks to Valerie and Carl Coons for putting up with me for all of these years, and for being the best grandparents anyone could ask for.

Thank-you to all of the friends and lovers who have inspired me along the way. You know who you are.

And one last thanks to you, the reader. Thank-you for supporting my work, and buying this book. In so doing you're making an implicit commitment to spend at least a couple hours of your life with me, and I recognize that's no small thing. So thank-you.

FOREWORD

I LIVE IN the top floor penthouse of an apartment building in the neighbourhood of El Poblado in Medellín, Colombia. It doesn't feel quite as exotic or grandiose as it might sound, but it is beautiful. I am surrounded by mountains covered in green, and after it rains, which it did this afternoon, it smells as if everything is clean and new and blooming for the first time.

The night I arrived in this city a few months ago, I attended one of the most intense parties of my life. I began writing this book at that party.

I had just spent a lengthy and uneventful night in an airport in Quito, Ecuador, and I desperately needed a hot shower and a quiet bedroom. I was thinking about this when I arrived at my hostel in Medellín, backpack in hand, following a bus ride down from the mountains at breakneck speeds. It was about 8 pm when I arrived in the city, and when I went to a local pub to ask for walking directions to my hostel, I could tell that something big was brewing.

It turned out that the local football team was about to win the league championship, and the entire city seemed captivated by the action. There were huge roars when the club scored, and piercing "OOOOOOOHs" when the opposing team came close to doing the same. Every person in every bar on the main strip was glued to a television set, and the cool night air felt charged with the energy of a massive forthcoming fiesta. I soon realized that it would be several hours before I could sleep.

There was a pretty, though plain-looking American girl in my hostel bedroom when I walked in. I avoided the typical traveler questions when I introduced myself ("Where are you from? How long have you been traveling?"), but I could tell she was American. Aside from the accent, many American female travellers have an air of presumed invincibility about them, and move from room to room with the confidence of a queen who thinks she owns the place. I quickly forgave her for this, however, because she was both decent looking, and a decent conversationalist. After a few minutes I invited her out on the town to catch the festivities. It seemed to be one of those nights you really shouldn't miss.

We dined on Mexican food at a rooftop restaurant overlooking the main square as the local team clinched their victory. When the game's final buzzer rang through the television it was as if every adult in the city shared one giant, euphoric orgasm; there were screams and roars and couples embracing and kissing each other, and very soon the American and I were dragged into the action on the street.

It was a little like I imagine "V-J Day" to have been on the streets of New York City, only with more rum and less anti-Japanese propaganda. The girl and I began to dance with the crowd and yell with the other revellers and drink copious amounts of the local spirits being offered to us from every direction.

I like stereotyping nationalities with positive qualities because it's quick and easy and it makes for interesting conversations with avowed racists and bigots. That said: Colombians are the most generous people I've ever encountered, and I formed this impression in the midst of that party. Everyone, it seemed, was toting massive bottles of rum and *aguardiente* (or "firewater") and pouring it down their neighbour's throat, and my friend and I were no exception. The streets of the main square were jam-packed, and it appeared that even the police were taking full advantage of the moment to get down and have one hell of a good time.

Within an hour of the football game's final buzzer it seemed as if Medellín had been hit by a massive snowfall. The tree-lined streets, and every unfortunate vehicle parked on them was coated with a fine white powder. Just about everyone drinking and dancing and partying on the street was taking handfuls of corn starch and either throwing it at the people in front of them, or hoisting it into the air, watching it rain down like New England snow. (If you've ever seen photos from India during the springtime festival of Holi, you'll begin to understand what I'm talking about.) Shortly after we began to walk around, my companion and I looked like we had just spent the evening with Tony Montana toward the end of *Scarface*. I struggled to see through the caked white powder covering my face. I looked to my right and saw that the American seemed to get it even worse than I did.

I quickly became drunk, and so did my companion. I was exhausted beyond words, having not slept in two days, but somehow I didn't care. Every face I encountered on the street seemed happy to see me; every bar we entered we found ten new friends. There were hugs and kisses and dancing and conversations in broken Spanish and I felt peaceful and energized and inspired. As the night wore on, the streetlights burned brighter, the music got louder, the girl got prettier, and I was damned glad to have landed in this city, that night. Sometimes the universe dumps a good party in your lap and you owe it to yourself, and the people around you, to reach out and grab it with both hands.

In the midst of that party, I began to think about how I might experience a similar type of vibrancy, joy, and celebration in my daily life, and share it with others. I started thinking about all the lessons I'd learned over the past few years that allowed me to become happier than I'd ever been before.

I thought about how most of the time we neglect the party going on around us all day, every day. We don't realize that we have the ability to indulge in our own personal party, and share our party with others, whenever we want. We forget that life—mundane, predictable, typical daily life—can be a celebration, if we choose. I don't need to wait until the local football team wins again to party as hard as I did the night I landed in Medellín, and neither do you.

As the streets cleared out and the sun came up, I realized that I really didn't want that party to stop. And for me, several months afterward, it hasn't.

. . .

BEFORE YOU DECIDED to pick up this odd little book, chances are good that you asked yourself at least one of the following two questions:

1.) What would some writer know about happiness that hasn't been written before?

2.) Why should I listen to him?

Fair questions, both.

With regards to the first question: probably very little. And my response to the second: you shouldn't.

Let me explain:

Some of the ideas and perspectives regarding life, death, and happiness which I present in this book will be familiar to you. Philosophers have been proposing similar courses of action for several millennia (though—I hope—not using the same tone or organization I have employed here). The Bible claimed there was "nothing new under the sun" about two thousand years ago, and it probably remains true today. However, that isn't to say that we can't inject new life into old ideas, and discover some exciting new possibilities in the process.

And secondly: I do not expect unconditional trust. Indeed, I would advise that you do *not* trust me until my words and your experiences line up. With this book it is more my intention to entertain, inflame, and inspire, than it is instruct. At the very least, I hope you can trust that these are the perspectives and practices that work for me, and have worked for many (many) others since the dawn of time.

I wrote this book, in part, to chronicle my experiences with joy, and the truths that I've discovered regarding happiness, with the hope that it might inspire my older self in the decades to come. I know too many people in their fifties and sixties who seem to have lost the twinkle in their eyes; lost that spark that moves one to get out of bed in the morning in eager anticipation of the day. And so they trudge through the day with neither joy nor pleasure, either taking comfort in former glories or forgetting those glories altogether. I fear the same happening to myself in the future, and thus, I want to remember how I feel and what I've discovered right now. And so, this is my truth:

I'm happy. Not all of the time, but most of the time. I experience real and profound joy on a daily basis; my life is full of bliss. I'm happy and I think each and every human being on earth deserves to be happy, and thus, I want to share some of my happiness with you, as well as my future self. There are a lot of unhappy people on the planet, and it seems exciting to share some of the joy that I've discovered with them. Hence, my desire to write this book, and engage with you.

Regardless of who you are and why you bought this book, I'm confident that the perspectives and practices I outline herein will help you to achieve more joy, peace of mind, and happiness on a consistent basis. I believe that this book has something to offer you, irrespective of your age, gender, income, location, or any other unimportant category. For one of the central truths of life is this: the rules concerning happiness, freedom, and living in greater harmony with ourselves and our neighbours are universal. I believe that if something works for me, it could and can work for you too. Whoever you are, and whatever your station in life, what we have in common is far greater, and more powerful, than what distinguishes us from each other.

I originally conceived of this book as a conversation. Indeed, I hope I get letters from readers who want to challenge me and my ideas, or tell me to go to hell, or explain how they employed these principles and practices in their own lives. This book was also inspired by a number of late night conversations with friends and lovers and family members, and thus, you will encounter their voices in our conversation also.

There is a wonderful bit by the comedian Louis CK in which he confesses to deploring the North American habit of small talk. He talks about encountering a chatty neighbour in the elevator, and is forced into a conversation about the weather:

"Let's talk about some *shit*," he says. "I always want to start conversations that way. [Let's] just get right to the talking. It's always disappointing to me when people talk about the weather because that means they didn't really want to talk about anything... [But] what if you didn't do that? *What if you didn't cop out?*"

I too have little patience for small talk. I'm from Canada, where talking about the weather, past, present, and future, often feels like a compulsory national pastime. Every morning my grandmother records the day's weather on her calendar. Every. Single. Morning. For as long as I can remember. Why? I've never asked. It's probably because she loves knowing about, talking about, and anticipating the weather just like 35 million other Canadians.

Of course there's nothing wrong with that, but I don't want to talk to you about the weather, and if we ever meet in person you'll discover the same. At dinner parties, I make a habit of ramping up the conversation to topics like love, sex, and the origins and ultimate fate of the universe when the conversation starts to veer towards rain and dry spells. Why? It's not because I'm a consummate prick (or so I tell myself). I do it because there's no time. I think life is too short to not consider the big questions, and ask others about their perspective on what really matters.

As I wrote this book, I was imagining having a late night chat with someone like me—someone who is or was forced to confront some serious personal demons before they felt able to achieve greater peace and happiness. If that's you, welcome. If it's not, of course you're welcome here too. Whoever you are, I'm grateful for your patronage, and attention.

Let's talk about some *shit*.

INTRODUCTION

WHAT DOES IT MEAN TO PARTY?

THIS IS A book about joy, but even that word seems inadequate. The word I'm looking for to sum up the spirit I want to write about doesn't exist, and that's probably a good thing; it's indescribable nature makes it even more mysterious and compelling, at least for me. What I'm interested in exploring are moments of pure and profound happiness--rapture and tranquility and life and death all wrapped up in one—and how to experience those moments on a more regular basis. This is what I mean when I use the word "joy." The French might call it *joie de vivre*, but we can stick with plain old "joy" for now.

I'm interested in moments when we lose ourselves to dance; when we are so completely present to our company on the dance floor, the music, and our body's reactionary vibrations that we forget, if only for a moment, our ego and our problems and our patience and our past and we have no choice but to submit to the bliss of the now.

I'm interested in those life-altering conversations at the bar with friends in which we realize, with exciting and unsettling clarity, who and what we really are behind our masks.

I'm interested in the serene bliss of orgasm; those moments when, wrapped around the body of another, we feel a piece of ourselves dying, letting go of our attachment to ourselves, and at the same time recognizing our unity with our partner and the universe and all things.

This is part of what I define as "joy."

I think life is—and should be treated as—one giant party. I believe that we have a sacred responsibility to bring the most possible light, love, and happiness to ourselves and the people around us at all times, and I believe in partying as a means to achieve just that. I know that life is meant to be lived, and lived intensely and thoroughly, right now. In a minute or two we will all be in a box in the ground, or settling on the funeral pyre, so I believe it is our duty as humans to party—and party very, very hard—in each and every moment of our lives.

As you can see, I take partying seriously. However, I don't use the word "partying" in the sense it is commonly understood.

I like "party" because most people associate the word with celebration, taking themselves and the world less seriously, and giving themselves permission to appreciate and enjoy life. However, the word is also associated with mindless, destructive, and juvenile behaviour. We may associate our own experience of "partying" with a few years in college, stumbling around campus bars and relying on alcohol and other drugs to loosen up and enjoy ourselves. Or perhaps we associate "partying" with happy hour at the local pub on a Friday night, unwinding after yet another long week of work. Or, we might only feel free to "party" when we take a vacation, grateful for the weeklong respite from our "regular lives" back home. Otherwise, we may permit ourselves to "party" just once a year at the office Christmas party, getting just drunk enough to finally take a pass at the secretary following several months of indecision.

For the most part, that isn't the "partying" I'm interested in.

The "partying" I refer to is about embracing life with as much rapturous joy and gratitude as is possible in any given moment. In every moment we have the opportunity to party, and seizing that opportunity can bring us closer to realizing our true nature as interconnected, infinitely-joyous beings. There is no bigger joy than in recognizing that we're all one, and I don't care how "new-agey" or flakey that statement might read. I know it to be true.

Freedom is found in the moment that you discover that your enjoyment of life, in every moment, depends almost entirely on your perspective; meaning is found in helping others realize the same. Combine the two, and you have my definition of enlightened partying.

We are so incredibly fortunate to have been born human, with our species' unique means and abilities to party, but we are far from the only entity on earth to do so. Have you ever witnessed the grace, energy, and beauty of dolphins swimming? Have you ever observed the intricate patterns and vibrant colours of moss growing on a tree? Have you ever watched bees swarming a hive? Or watched a raging river flow? The party is endless—look around.

So please consider "partying" in broad terms throughout this book. Lose your limited definition of partying (if you have one), and begin to think of the word and the principle as applicable in each and every situation throughout your everyday life; this is what I'm encouraging you to try with this book. In each and every moment you have the ability to choose to enjoy yourself, or not; to decide to party, or not. I think that choosing the former is always the best decision, for ourselves and for everyone around us. And you have abundant opportunities, each and every day:

Waiting in line at the bank can be a fantastic partying opportunity; perhaps there is someone wearing a bizarre hat standing behind you who you could engage in conversation. Think about it for a moment—each and every human being on earth has had an enormous variety of experiences and knowledge of which you are entirely ignorant. Everyone is fascinating. Everyone has a little joy, or a little humour, or a little lesson to share with you that has the potential to enrich your life, as you enrich theirs. Simply put: everyone is a party.

A select few beings on Earth have stumbled on an immensely valuable, often overlooked secret to attaining happiness. The secret is this: work is a party. Every job, every occupation, every profession a fiesta. Every coworker, every boss—no matter how obnoxious or assholeian—has something to teach you, about yourself and about the world. And you can choose to use your labour as an excuse to party. So step into your body, go deep into your work, and experience it fully, for one day you will never have the opportunity to make such a contribution. No labour is inherently "deadening;" every profession that contributes, in however tiny a way, to the betterment and sustenance of our planet deserves praise and respect. You, too, can give your labour the respect it deserves, and make the decision to enjoy yourself while you perform it.

Being stuck in traffic can be absolutely wonderful. As you wait in your car, you have a wide variety of music at your disposal which you now have a prime opportunity to dive into, completely uninterrupted. This is a chance to plunge into sounds and melody and rhythm and immerse yourself in art. Many people never get the opportunity; you do. So dance, thrash, rave, whatever. Or simply sit still, close your eyes, and absorb the vibrations. It's magic.

Walking your dog is another great chance to party. Think about it—you are taking a beautiful animal for exercise so that its life will be happier and longer, as will your own. What's more: the animal loves you without reservation. There is solid earth beneath your feet, and you can explore any avenue you choose. It doesn't matter if you're exploring new territory in the neighbourhood, or walking a path you've walked a thousand times before, your dog is totally absorbed in the journey; you can be, too. Furthermore, you have three things:

1.) Ample free time to engage in leisure activities such as walking the dog

2.) Enough income to sustain not only yourself with food, water, and shelter, but also another living being

3.) The physical health to walk for extended periods of time

The majority of human beings who have ever lived lacked at least one of those three things. You aren't simply "walking the dog;" you are engaged in a rare and precious experience of being human not afforded to the majority of our planet's past and current inhabitants. Savour it.

As you can see, enlightened partying can take place in your living room, in your car, at a restaurant, on a beach, in bed, in an airplane, in the shower, or on the toilet. Our party is everywhere; this party is versatile.

Enlightened partying is largely about gratitude—gratitude for the moment, gratitude for living, gratitude for others, gratitude for the opportunity to experience real and intense joy in any moment you choose. But it's also about recognizing your rights—recognizing that you have the *right* to be happy. You have the right to choose happiness in any given moment, regardless of the circumstances. You have the right to party all the time.

Furthermore, you have the ability to party so hard that you experience real enlightenment. Enlightenment isn't about sitting quietly in a room for twenty years waiting for something big to happen to your brain. Enlightenment is about recognizing your ultimate truth: recognizing the false nature and empty promise of your ego, and your ultimate unity with all things. Each and every being on earth is simply a different aperture of the universe, looking at and experiencing itself. You are not John Smith—you *are* the Big Bang.

I believe that partying can help us realize this. I believe that experiencing moments of real and pure and transcendent bliss can bring us closer to enlightenment—closer to realizing that we are all one, if only for a moment, and eventually closer to experiencing the peace and joy of *knowing* that we are all one at all times.

I'm not saying it's easy—sometimes it is, but sometimes it *really* isn't.

I am fortunate to be blessed with parents who love me, a wide network of supportive and interesting friends, inspiring female companionship, enough income to live comfortably, the ability to travel the world, and a profession I enjoy and take endless inspiration from. Even though I have been so lucky, sometimes I find it difficult to muster the partying spirit I describe in this book. Ask anyone—sometimes I can be an absolute *bastard* to be around.

Many lack some or all of the blessings I just listed, and many have far more. Whatever your situation, we all occasionally face difficulty in mustering up the energy or inclination to party.

The real trick is to party on, even in the most dire of circumstances and challenging of situations. It isn't easy, but your party muscle will grow stronger and stronger each and every time you choose happiness over despair; optimism over hopelessness; gratitude over resentment; having a good time, over simply "killing time." Over the years, I've found that enlightened partying gets easier—and more rewarding—with continued practice.

So wherever you are as you read these words, take a moment to party right now. Breathe deeply, feel your feet on the ground, and step into your body. Forget the past, forget the future. Let go of your ego; let go of that voice inside telling you who you are, and what you should do, and what's the "proper" thing to do or feel in this moment. Right now, you are blessed with the opportunity to party—seize it.

Let's move.

1. DEATH

TONIGHT A GOOD man died, and I don't use that adjective lightly.

When I met him he had a plump nose, a frizzled patch of thin grey hair, and drooping, peach-grey ears. He wore no glasses, and his eyes seemed to be at least one size too small to match the rest of his face. He walked slow but proud, and it was clear that his sense of wonder had not aged along with his body. He asked you questions, and you could tell he was genuinely curious to know the answer. He had a funny little smile which he revealed while regaling visitors with tales from his life which were at least half true. (Does it really matter, in the end?)

When he was a young man the President and the newspaper and most of the people he knew told him to join the fight against the Japanese. So he did, but soon he decided to trade his gun for a camera.

He became a skilled and original artist, photographing people, places, and major events around the world well into his eighties. Whether he was capturing fighter pilots in their final moments, or Parisien street children along the canal, he knew when and how to catch his subjects so that they were truly revealed.

He traveled from a battleship in the Pacific to Europe, Africa, Asia, and all over the United States. In later life he had children, and though they always wanted more from him, he gave them what he could. Like most men, he had difficulty negotiating his purpose in life with children, family, commitment.

He liked women, even when he was old and frail, and he was unabashed regarding the same. I like that quality in men. I'm not sure if there's a God, but if there is, I believe the presence of women on our planet is the best evidence of His gender. Their beauty covers the earth, making every city and town brighter in its own way; I respect other men who acknowledge and celebrate that. That said, his like of women extended to women beyond his wife, and because of that his family suffered.

His impact is written on the faces of his children and grandchildren, and every woman he once loved. His photographs will live on and inspire long after his death. And all of the rooms and houses and places he inhabited —everything he saw—will be forever marked by his presence. Every grain of sand, every beach, every dense forest and every city street he touched is richer because he once lived. He's dead, but his energy remains.

His legacy is rich and messy and painful and beautiful and strange and incomplete and at the same time perfect. For he lived, and lived a full, and adventurous life. He loved living, and the people around him loved him for it.

...

YOU MAY FIND it strange or ironic that Chapter One of a book about joy is concerned with death, but I don't.

From the day that *Everyday Joy* began to take shape, I knew that this had to be the first chapter. If our aim is to cultivate more joy in life, it is essential to consider death.

Death is at the core of real joy. A vague sense of oncoming death is at the core of every great party. Death watches over everything, providing each and every partier with an unconscious awareness that this party may well be their last.

Many people choose to either ignore, or vilify death. Our primary cultural signifier of death is that of the shadowy grim reaper, wearing a skeletal face and black robes, anticipating our demise with glee.

The topic of death is brought up at a dinner party, and guests shy away and try to change the topic to something more "upbeat," and less "depressing."

An elderly family member dies and the funeral home director spends hours applying makeup and pressing an old suit; doing everything in his power to spare us—the living—from witnessing the reality of post-mortem decay.

Most people spend their lives trying to ignore the spectre of death like some beggar in the street, pretending not to notice, pretending not to hear the steady rhythm of death's footsteps following their own. I have never understood why.

There is no other thought that inspires, excites, and motivates me like the thought of my own death. No other idea that pushes me to achieve, and achieve now. Nothing motivates me to party like the image of death I see in my head, watching my body burn on the funeral pyre; decaying with a peaceful grin on my face, saddened that one party is ending, but at the same time curious about the next.

We all grow up knowing one thing, and one thing only: we are born, and one day we will die. That's it. That is the only bonafide, 100-proof, absolute certainty about life and living that we have access to. This is the only thing we know for sure. It is ironic, then, that we spend most of our lives trying to forget it.

I know some people who express a desire to live forever. But people who think they want to live forever rarely ask themselves an important question: do I even *want* to?

Immortality would be pure hell. Do you want to go around and around and around on the same Ferris wheel for all time? Think about it.

Spinning around on this rock in the same form for all eternity would become painfully dull after a century or two. What makes our time on Earth so exciting is that it is a limited time offer. At a certain point, we all have to step off to make room for whoever is coming up behind us. This is what makes the ride so exciting, and entertaining any thoughts to the contrary spoils it for ourselves, and for all of the other passengers onboard.

It's useful to think long and hard about your death if you want to live, and I don't mean the funeral arrangements. I mean your *actual* death, not the after-party.

When the hour of your death draws near, how do you think you'll feel? How do you want to feel? What thoughts are you going to hold close as you slip away? We all die alone, but do you want a stranger or loved ones to witness your departure? In your final moments will you choose to stay present, or speculate about what will come next?

My ultimate aspiration in life is to die happy, and to die well. I imagine an aged and weathered body—mine— breathing slowly and achy, laying on a firm mattress with a solid oak bed frame draped in white linens, with an open window revealing a perfect late September evening and a cool fall breeze. I want to be surrounded by a gorgeous family and loving eyes, gentle witnesses to my transition. I picture a peaceful grin on my face as my pain and joy and problems and passions and money and sex and health all fade to black, and all of a sudden, there is nothing. I take one, final breath, and I am gone, never to return in the same form.

As I move on from this earthly form I want to die having really lived; to have sucked as much bliss and joy and excitement out of my time on Earth as humanly possible. To die happy is to die knowing that I brought as much light, love and happiness to myself and the people around me as I was capable. To die wearing a wide smile on my face, with multiple wrinkles around my eyes revealing ten thousand afternoons spent laughing with friends, my voice hoarse following ten thousand wild nights and conversations, my limbs tired after a century of dance. I want to die in absolute peace so that my rest is eternal, and those witnesses to my death are inspired to keep living, and living well.

Death is exciting, and not because of some speculative and imaginary afterlife, but because it provides the ultimate excuse to live, and live now. To exercise every passion and exorcise every demon, to pursue each and every curious avenue, and dive into the ocean of joy that stands at your feet in every moment of every day.

We delude ourselves, and cheat ourselves and others out of joy when we live in deliberate ignorance of death. When we ignore death it draws nearer. So what is the solution?

Consider this frequently: **you will die.**

Move deeply into death. Try to imagine the sights, sounds, and smells of the room where you will die.

Imagine the thoughts you will have as the music fades and the lights grow dim. Picture your diminishing body, slowly voiding itself of life as death moves in. Picture the people around you (if there are any) as they watch. Imagine their faces, and try to listen to their voices, as you imagine your own. Will you speak? Will you smile? *How do you want to die?*

As you read these words and follow this narrative, you are nearer to death than when you began. What's more, death may come at any moment. Each and every day many thousands of people around the world die long before they anticipated. Death is so near that you can actually hear it, if it's quiet enough and your mind is still. In every moment, there is a very real chance that your time on Earth will end; death follows our every movement as human beings.

So make no mistake: your party *will* end. Your breath is not eternal. Your flesh will one day rot and decay so that your corpse will be unrecognizable to everyone you once cared about, and who once cared for you. If you choose to buried in a hole in the ground, your flesh will eventually return whence it came, the mould and the bugs and the worms and the bacteria consuming the physical evidence of your life so that their lives can go on. If you choose to be cremated, your body will turn to ash, with hot reams of fire igniting your hair and skin and bones so that you eventually fit into a neat metal box to be carried around and eventually disposed of by friends and family. You may end up in the Ganges, or Lake Minnetonka, but the end result is the same.

You will die. And not only will you die, but everyone you love and who loves you will also die. Furthermore, one day, whether it is in one hundred or one hundred thousand years, there will be no memory, trace, or evidence that you once lived.

So what are you to do about it?

Live.

Live, and live now. Live powerfully, dramatically, absolutely now. Live with as much gusto and passion and strength as you can muster. And don't stop until you are so absolutely satisfied with living that death seems a curious, even welcome, transition.

Party now. Party so hard, so wantonly, that you can die having known the most joy any human has ever experienced in life. Party so that the walls of the rooms you inhabited will forever reverberate with your energy. Party so that other, less enlightened partiers give themselves permission to party too. Party all the way to the end; party on your deathbed.

Live fully now because you will never get another chance.

2. FUNERALS

YES, FOLLOWING A chapter about death, I'm asking you to think about funerals. It too is essential, if you're interested in living a joyous, fulfilling life. It, too, can be enormously motivating, and inspiring.

I am far from the first writer to make such a request of his readership. Men and women throughout history have encouraged the same, and there's a very good reason for it: it sharpens the mind to what is important in a hurry.

So try it: as you considered your own death and dying in the previous chapter, imagine what your funeral might look and sound like were you to die tomorrow.

Who would attend your funeral? Who wouldn't? Who would be most impacted by your death? Who would deliver your eulogy? What might they say? Ask yourself: what are the words that others would use to describe you, and sum up the life you lived?

Take a moment and get a clear picture in your head. Imagine you're a fly on the wall, observing your own casket and the behaviour of everyone surrounding it. What is the general atmosphere in the room?

Once you're clear about what it might look and feel like, I ask: how do you feel about your funeral? Are you satisfied with the proceedings? Are you disappointed with the eulogy? How do you feel about the general portrait of you, and your life, painted by the attendees?

Many funerals are morose and uninspiring. Many funerals feature humourless men and women describing the humourless departed with about as much enthusiasm as one might reserve for a pair of wet socks. Everyone eats a couple of mediocre sandwiches and returns home deflated. It's more than a little depressing.

A couple of years ago I began thinking about my own funeral. I attempted to answer the same questions I asked you above, and very quickly I became dissatisfied with the general theme of the answers.

I looked in the mirror and saw a man who others might describe as closed off, aloof, a little too self-satisfied and not nearly as much fun as he imagines himself to be. I imagined the people at my funeral remembering a man who they never really got to know all that well, however much they once wanted to. I pictured an unsatisfying eulogy. I imagined friends and family members leaving out some of the adjectives to describe me that I might have once hoped for. Words like:

Generous.

Energetic.

Kind.

Appreciative.

Inspiring.

Fun-loving.

Loving.

When I began to speculate about my funeral, I started to get more clear about the gifts that I wanted to offer the world before my time on this rock is over. I began to know, instinctively, the personal characteristics that I want to be remembered for when I die. I decided that I had to start investing more time into having a good time, and sharing my good time with others. In short: I realized how important it was to live a more joyous, and generous life, before I no longer have the opportunity.

I asked you those questions because I think you too can gain clarity about your priorities when considering the answers. You too can arrive at some uncomfortable conclusions about who and what you are in the current moment. You too can come to some exciting, clarifying, and motivating conclusions about who and what you want to be tomorrow. You too can strive to be remembered as an individual for whom life was a party, and one who worked hard to bring as much fun, love, and joy to others as you were capable.

Forget the depressing black suits, and sombre speeches: your funeral can be a party. Your funeral can be an opportunity for others to honour, celebrate, and draw inspiration from a life well lived, rather than a dry and dreary commemoration of your passing. Which sounds better to you?

I want the commemoration of my death to be injected with the same vibrant spirit I exhibited in life. I want my funeral to inspire others to live. When I die I want my funeral to be a party which I regret being unable to attend in person.

So I'll ask once more: how do you want to be remembered? What are the personal characteristics and qualities which are most important to you to be remembered for in death? What do you want your funeral to look like? How does your eulogy read?

This last question is important, and I propose that you complete the following exercise in order to get clear about your ideal life in a hurry:

Write your ideal eulogy. Pick a friend or family member who might deliver it, and write out—in their voice, and in as much or as little detail as you wish—how you want them to remember you. Take a week, take an hour, but however long it takes make sure you sit down and give it some thought. It's worthwhile, I promise you.

Once you're clear about what you want to be remembered for, the question becomes: **how are you going to make it happen?**

Which experiences and characteristics in life do you want to aspire to so that you are remembered, and remembered fondly, in death? What do you need to do right now so that your funeral is inspiring, and motivating to others? What are the gifts you need to share with the world so that your legacy is guaranteed?

However your imaginary eulogy reads, I can almost guarantee one thing: if you chose to read this book, having the best time possible is important to you. Experiencing and sharing cosmic, transformational joy matters to you, as it should.

We die a little each and every time we cheat ourselves out of happiness. Over time, if we continue this pattern, the spark in our eyes begins to fade so much that eventually barely any light remains. Our soul begins to wither and close in on itself, and the impact we have on others becomes limited. We become isolated, alone in our patience and discontent, waiting for "good things" to happen to us instead of creating them for ourselves.

I want to be remembered as a man for whom a good time was a consistent, even compulsory aspect of life. A man who actively sought out, and created his own party on a daily basis. A man who, even in challenging circumstances, chose happiness over despair, action over inaction, living well over simply living. A man who knew that his default setting as a human being was to be happy, and helped others realize the same.

I want my funeral to inspire everyone in attendance to cultivate more joy in their own lives. I want every attendee to return home feeling a little more optimistic about life, and the infinite possibilities they can aspire to, and experience in life. I want to leave behind a messy, motivating, imperfect and compelling story for others to look at and say "Wow. He *really* lived."

What about you?

3. PAIN

IN NOVEMBER OF 2008 I spent the majority of my days sitting cross legged on the cold floor of a meditation hall in northern India. I was living in the woods outside of a tiny Himalayan village called Dharamkot, surrounded by cedar trees and mountains and little else, attending a meditation retreat for the first time in my life. Like many other areas of my life, when I first became interested in meditation I dove in headfirst, signing up for a 10-day silent retreat during which I would be cut off from the outside world, and meditating for somewhere north of ten hours a day. It was intense, especially for someone with limited previous experience with meditation.

After the first or second day of the retreat, my legs began to numb each time I took my seat on the floor of the meditation hall. By day three this numbness was replaced by a severe pain shooting up the left side of my body. The practice required sitting as still as possible, so I was determined not to shift my position to ease the pain overtaking my left leg.

I can be a stubborn individual. When I set my mind to something my resolve to see it through is unwavering, and I was committed to this meditation; I was committed to maintaining perfect posture, and stilling my wandering mind, regardless of my discomfort.

But on that particular day all I could focus on was the pain. My body simply wasn't used to sitting on the ground for hours at a time while trying to remain motionless. I remembered that the teacher mentioned that, should the pain become unbearable, students were permitted to shift their position, but I wasn't having it. I was going to do this meditation thing right, damn it, pain or no pain.

The pain grew worse. I began to sweat and curse myself for signing up for such a crazy experiment. I became agitated, edgy, and miserable. I proceeded to fantasize about how incredible it would feel to get up, and relieve the unbearable cramps I now felt throughout the lower half of my body. What bliss, I imagined. What absolute bliss.

"I can walk outside and massage and stretch my legs and breathe in the cool, clean mountain air and it will feel wonderful," I thought. "I may even go to bed early… It's insane that we have to get up at 4:45 every morning. Absolutely insane."

The throbbing continued, only now it felt like my whole leg was swelling up and vibrating to the rhythm of my heart beat. It was a bizarre and dramatic cocktail of pain. I wasn't sure if I had signed up for a meditation retreat, or some Indian prisoner of war camp.

My sweating grew worse.

"This place is a prison," I thought. "It's like the world's most mellow, enlightened prison. This is hell, this sitting on the floor for eleven hours a day... It's ridiculous...I'm going outside."

I was just about to cave—juuuuust about to get up, and get the hell out of that hall in order to take a walk and ease the pain in my legs—when it struck me:

I can decide to observe this pain.

Right now I'm choosing to react to it, but I don't have to. I can just observe it, like a doctor might observe a patient.

Because this pain isn't bad or miserable or anything—this pain simply is. It's just physical sensations. I'm deciding to freak out over it, but it's completely unnecessary. Right now I'm letting it have power over my mood, but it doesn't necessarily have that right... I'm offering pain the power to dictate how I feel. Maybe I can strip pain of its right to impact how I feel. Maybe I can strip pain of its power by not reacting to it.

I'm bigger than this pain. So maybe I can just watch it, rather than react to it.

My meditation practice at the time was all about observation—observing my body's natural pattern of respiration, as well as the physical sensations that cover my body—but I didn't really appreciate or understand it until that moment. In that moment, I had a revelation:

Even in the midst of intense physical pain, we can choose not to react to it. Real pain doesn't come from the actual physical sensation of discomfort—real pain comes from our *aversion* to that discomfort. In other words, the way we react to the pain is far worse than the pain itself. What is painful is our usual response *to* pain.

A deep sense of equanimity came over me, and I remained completely still. I remained totally present to the discomfort that had overtaken my left leg, only now I wasn't reacting to it. I began to watch it, as one might observe a painting in a museum. "Oh, that's interesting," I thought to myself. "Now it feels like my leg is buzzing, when before it was throbbing. Interesting. Interesting."

I stopped sweating and panicking and cursing myself, and I remained still. The pain no longer bothered me, and I carried on with my meditation practice. Eventually, the pain began to fade, then fade some more, and then it was gone.

This experience changed me at a deep level. This experience altered the way I respond to pain and discomfort of all kinds. I cannot overstate the value that that sweaty leg pain brought to my life.

Pain—any kind of pain—isn't what we think it is. Pain isn't nasty, or awful, or scary, or disgusting, or unpleasant, or powerful—these are just words we attribute to our aversion to, and attempted avoidance of the pain. Pain is just pain. We are the ones who ascribe meaning and significance to it; without this, pain is impotent.

For a period following my experience at the meditation retreat, I experimented with my discovery in a variety of fashions. I would pinch my arm until it bled in order to exercise my ability to observe pain. I would contort the lower half of my body in all sorts of uncomfortable positions in order to practice. I would try to think of the most painful and uncomfortable conversations and interactions of my past, and play them out in my head over and over again, going deep into the shame, guilt, and embarrassment I once felt.

You don't have to take it that far to recognize your own ability to observe pain. Instead, just try this:

Make a conscious decision to observe, rather than react to your pain.

That's it. Just make up your mind.

You have the ability to interpret, and respond to, any experience in life in whichever manner you choose. No matter how painful or undesirable the experience, you have the power to decide how to react, or not to react.

You will face real and intense pain throughout your life. You will experience enormous losses, debilitating setbacks, and serious hardships of every sort. You have probably already experienced real pain.

But the party goes on. Life goes on. No matter your situation in life—no matter how painful your current reality—you have the ability and the right to enjoy yourself. You have the ability, the right, and—I believe—the responsibility to party, even in the midst of hardship and pain. Because you are alive.

You are alive. And no person, no event, and no thing has the right to impede on your ability to enjoy yourself. The Beastie Boys got it wrong—you don't have to "fight for your right to party." You always have it; it is *always* an option.

The question then becomes: HOW do I exercise my right to party in the midst of hardship and pain? How can I enjoy myself even in the midst of enormous setbacks and debilitating losses?

You can decide to challenge, and eventually shift your perspective on those events and circumstances.

Most of our greatest learning as humans comes from painful experiences. Pain is perhaps our greatest teacher about the world, about others, about ourselves. Pain gives us new perspective about our own strength; pain builds us up. Pain forces us to test and strengthen our party muscle. Pain teases and taunts us, as a good-intentioned sports coach might, until we are bigger, better, stronger because of it. Pain is our ally; we should love pain.

Pain isn't easy, but that's the point—it isn't *supposed* to be easy. Whether we lose our leg or lose our girlfriend, pain forces us to grow, and become stronger people. If pain were meant to be inviting and delicious it would be called "pina colada," or something like that, but it isn't. It's pain, and it is an essential aspect of our humanity.

We wouldn't know pleasure without pain. For most of us, pleasure is easy—whether we're sitting at the beach with a loved one, or watching the game on a Sunday afternoon, pleasure is nice. Pleasure is fun. But how could we recognize it without pain?

If life were nothing but pleasure it wouldn't be pleasurable. We would take it for granted and soon it would become tedious, like a bad dream we couldn't wake up from. We would all try very hard to seek out pain just to know something different. And when we couldn't find it, suicide would become the next logical step in order to escape such a predictable, uninteresting, and unchallenging existence.

We wouldn't be humans without pain—life would not be life without it—and we can choose to deal with it however we want.

We have a choice. We can be afraid of pain, nervously anticipate it, and try to avoid it all costs, or we can choose something different. We can accept it. We can embrace it. We can observe it. We can do whatever we want with it; that is our power. Pain is not inherently good or bad—pain simply is. We decide the rest.

And thus we can, if we choose, party through the pain. We can decide:

"Yes, pain is present, and I choose to accept and observe and party in the midst of it, because I can respond to it however I want."

Anyone who chooses to observe, rather than react to pain, discovers a wonderful secret: you strip pain of its power in the process. Pain is no longer intimidating; pain is no longer painful, and thus, our freedom expands. Our ability to party grows stronger.

So welcome pain, observe pain, don't be averse to pain, and don't fear pain. Pain is. That's all.

Make the decision to party through your pain because it is the best option, for yourself and for everyone around you. Because when you decide to party through your pain, others see that they can party through theirs, too.

4. DRUGS

FOR THE ENTIRETY of my adult life, and a good bit of my teens, alcohol has been my drug of choice. There is something about that warm glow—usually around my second glass of wine—that I find delightful. Whether I choose to take in the evening at home, spending some quality time with Miles Davis or Shostakovich or Hemingway or Hitchcock, or am out on the town with friends, a drink or two often adds value to my life, and bolsters my inclination to party.

I still remember the first time I got drunk.

I was 15, at a house party filled with older teens, many of them of my co-workers from the grocery store. I drank five or six bottles of Budweiser, and all of a sudden everyone's jokes got a little funnier, and we all laughed a little harder. It was as if God had turned the volume up on the world, and made everything seem a little more abrasive and interesting. To make matters even more interesting, someone put on the film *Fear and Loathing in Las Vegas*, and we all watched in silence, captives to the surreal glow emanating from the television. (Yes, I had my first extended experience with both alcohol and Hunter S. Thompson in the same night. It was fantastic.)

You'll notice that I'm leaving out the part about my first real hangover the next morning. (Thank god for mothers who serve strong coffee and scrambled eggs.) My point is this: for as long as I've taken one, a drink or two usually loosens me up and opens my senses to allow greater appreciation of the moment. I can read Hemingway, and hear the guns and see the bridge and almost picture the front lines. I can listen to Shostakovich and almost trace the source of his magic. I can dance all night; my slight intoxication nullifying any remaining self-consciousness or self-seriousness on the dance floor. I can embrace my friends with total honesty, and I know that alcohol has given birth to many of the most intimate, and revealing conversations of my life.

As I write to you this evening I am sitting on a rooftop patio, watching the sun set over the Andes foothills just before dusk, listening to birds chirp above me, sipping on a Colombian rum with a twist of lime, feeling wonderful. This view. Those birds. This rum. Could I appreciate my current surroundings with equal enthusiasm were I sober? Perhaps. But there *is* something about this drink—something in its essence as it enters my bloodstream allows me to breathe a little more deeply, look a little harder, listen a little more carefully, and soak it all in just a tiny bit more.

For milennia, our species has utilized—and in many cases relied on—alcohol as a means to inspire, inaugurate, and enhance celebrations of every sort. I've often been guilty of the same. Whether I'm out on the town with a lady companion, or at the pub with friends, I often rely on alcohol to better enjoy my company and the celebration at hand.

And it makes sense: for myself and for most people, alcohol relaxes, entertains, and encourages us to let down our masks to reveal who and what we really are.

Growing up in rural Canada, alcohol felt like an essential prerequisite for my inauguration into manhood. Whether it was sharing my first beer with my father (and pretending to like the taste) at the tender age of 14, or purchasing my first case of beer at the illegal age of 16, or getting drunk with Hunter and the guys from the grocery, I associate alcohol with my formative years of adulthood.

Like most men, I encounter barriers to sharing emotional intimacy with other men. In high school, I had a very close friend with whom I felt a deep kinship and mutual love. I know he loved me because every once in a while he would tell me; however, only when we were drinking. I acted in a similar manner, scared to reveal how much his friendship meant to me when I was sober.

It's become an oft-repeated joke in movies and television, the drunk buddies slinging their arms over one another walking down the street, slurring "I love you, man," to each other after a fun night out. The audience knows it's true—their love is real—it's just that the alcohol renders them loose enough to be honest with each other about it. That's the joke, but I'm not sure it's funny.

Most men and women use alcohol as an excuse to let their love out. Surely, we have all come across a miserable drunk, but for myself and for most people, a little alcohol lets us smile a bit wider, laugh a bit harder, dance a bit freer, and love a little more honestly. And this is why it's so essential to learn to party with others while remaining sober.

I don't mean sober all the time. Were I to give up the drink entirely I would miss it as I would a dear and departed friend. I simply mean to encourage you to experiment with sober partying in social situations. I have tried it myself, and discovered some uncomfortable and revealing truths in the process.

For example: I am often more reserved, and less loving when I don't have alcohol as an excuse to relax in social situations. While sober, I'm often less honest and adventurous than I am when I've had a pint or two. I'm not the only person to make similar discoveries about themselves. Which begs the questions:

Why is alcohol so intimately associated with partying? Why do so many of us rely on alcohol to loosen up? What right does alcohol have to give us permission to party? Why are we often more honest, more intimate, more loving while drunk than sober? Why is it that for many people "sober partying" appears a boring, or even daunting prospect?

I think it's sad. I think it's sad and pathetic and a serious indictment of our society's restrictive views on partying, and the general appreciation and enjoyment of life. Part of what I hope to accomplish with this book is to challenge these limited ways of thinking about joy, and limit our reliance on alcohol or any other drug to party.

For drugs and partying are not inherently connected; indeed, alcohol has been known to fracture and destroy more than a few great celebrations. The truth is alcohol often serves as a "party crutch:" often, we only give ourselves permission to let loose and enjoy ourselves when alcohol is involved. This renders our party muscle weak and flabby, at the cost of lucid joy, and enlightened partying.

Alcohol can also serve as "party steroids:" it may amp up, and expand our party muscle on the surface, but deep beneath the muscle starves for proper nutrition and exercise in order to render it truly, organically, strong.

Sober partying is enlightened partying, and that's where the real payoff lies: in cultivating the ability to experience profound joy, hearty laughs, deep conversations, real connections, and true intimacy without the crutch of alcohol or any other substance.

You may think that alcohol makes yourself and others more interesting, but it doesn't: alcohol simply reveals what is already there, hidden just beneath your self-conscious surface, and theirs.

Alcohol is the most abused drug on the planet because humans have a deep-rooted need to party, and most humans associate partying with alcohol. For while it often lets us share our love, our joy, our party with the people around us, at a certain point we begin to rely on it to do so. This cheats ourselves and the people around us out of greater joy and communion when we are sober.

The good news is there is a solution. And the solution is enlightened partying.

When my party muscle is strong and well-exercised, and I can really tap into my naturally joyous spirit, sobriety comes naturally. And I can share the same love, joy, compassion, and fun with others while sober, or while drinking. The drink isn't the point—the party is.

When you begin to practice partying in everyday situations, partying sober at the bar doesn't seem like that much of a stretch. When you're sharing and encouraging the same light, love, and happiness with your friends at the bar as you do with the guy standing behind you in line at the bank, you start to realize how unnecessary alcohol is to having a good time. Your party is everywhere, with or without a drink in your hand.

So don't rely on alcohol as an excuse, or means to party. Alcohol can enhance a good party, but it can also destroy it. Furthermore, your reliance on it weakens your ability to party through life, and share that party with others each and every day.

When you can party just as hard with Dr. Pepper as you can with Jack Daniels, you will know that your party muscle is strong. You will be approaching Jedi levels of enlightened partying, and those partiers in your midst will be impressed, encouraged, and inspired by your abilities.

5. LONELINESS

WESTERN CULTURE IS obsessed with the intellect; convinced that our personality, our charm, our contribution to the betterment of our species occurs as a result of the effort of our brain. Convinced that, in the end, our intellect will save the planet from destruction. Convinced that our ego—our sense of self, of individuality and accomplishment—makes us who we are. If we exist as individuals at all, we think, surely our brain —our conscious mind, our ego— represents the seat of our personhood. And so we struggle.

Most of us go through life with a deep and unfulfilled longing for communion with other humans because we feel lonely, and trapped in our own heads. Our ego tells us that we are each unique, isolated individuals on a distinct journey from all other beings on Earth; a visitor to this planet, rather than a product of it. We feel like no one can understand us because everyone else is as limited by their own unique, ego-based perspective as we are.

In our attempts to quell this gnawing sense of isolation, we join religious organizations, cultivate a network of close friends and family members, and seek out romantic relationships. On some level we are convinced that these relationships will provide us with the intimate communion we so desperately seek, but we're wrong. After we join the church, or make a friend, or get the girl, we still feel alone, and can't figure out why.

"She doesn't understand me," we think to ourselves. "Why doesn't she give me what I need?" although we are unable to express exactly what those needs are in the first place. We might try to explain our needs in vague terms such as "intimacy," "desire," "love," "passion," or "commitment," but we are all basically saying the same thing: we want to feel less alone. We *always* want to feel less alone.

This sense of isolation can trace its roots to social conditioning, rather than our biology as humans. From the time we are born our parents and society and culture tells us that we are all, basically, freaks; isolated beings who, through either some galactic oddity or God-directed initiative, miraculously appeared on this planet at a certain point in time with unique strengths, abilities, weaknesses and demons, each of us different. We are one-time visitors to this planet with individual egos and physical features that distinguish us from all of the other visitors that came before, and will come in the future. We are told that we all come into, and depart this world alone; billions of strangers on billions of isolated journeys. Either cosmic flukes, or children of God counting the days until we return to His heavenly kingdom.

We all hunger to share intimacy with others without realizing that communion is hard-wired into our being from the moment of our conception. We don't realize that we each represent living parts of one giant whole, as opposed to individual visitors on limited-time only trips.

We are the sun and the moon and the stars and the Earth and the planets and the light and the dark of the cosmos all wrapped up in one. We are, each of us, an aperture of the universe looking at, and experiencing itself. Each of us is the planet, in a very real sense, and thus, we are as far from being isolated, cut-off visitors to this planet as could be possible. We are anything *but* alone.

It's all very well to read this in a book, or listen to a lecturer describe the same, but it isn't always easy to really feel it; really live with that knowledge deeply imprinted in your consciousness. There are various routes which make it easier to get there, and I believe that simply being present and living in your body, rather than your brain, is one of the most effective ones.

Why do millions of people around the world play sports every day? Why do we go for a run? Why do we go to the gym? Why do we have sex? Or meditate? Why do we go for a massage? Or go for a swim?

The answer to all of these questions is presence. Any activity that requires our full body's, and not just our brain's, participation immediately gets us away from the constant noise in our heads, and into our bodies. Any activity that requires our full body's engagement, alertness, and attention makes us feel more present; when we play sports or have sex, we become intensely engaged in the present moment. We partake in these activities for a variety of reasons, but one common reason is that they are all simple routes to presence.

We instinctively partake in activities that encourage presence because we are happiest when we are most present. Most meditators, participants in tantric sex, and professional athletes share a common characteristic: they feel happiest, and most at peace, when they are wholly engaged with the present moment as they give their gift and perform their craft. Thankfully, anyone can achieve this type of presence in any moment, and thus, we all have access to happiness in any given moment.

But most people feel like they can only experience this type of full-body, wholly-alert presence when they are meditating, or exercising, or having sex, or playing sports, etc. but they're wrong. Full body presence is possible in any moment, regardless of where you are or what you're doing.

For centuries, students of Zen have been cultivating this ability. Teachers of Zen challenge their students to be intensely engaged in whatever they are doing, in any given moment. In Zen, if one is tasked with washing the dishes, one is to wash the dishes and be conscious of nothing else. It then becomes possible to lose yourself, and shed the illusion of your ego, in the act of washing. Meditation is *not* reserved to sitting on the floor and being quiet. It is preached that life itself should be one long meditation, whether we are practicing walking meditation, singing meditation, laughing meditation, driving meditation, or washing-the-dishes meditation.

So try this: after you finish reading this chapter, meditate on whatever task you perform next. Whether it is washing the dishes, walking down the street, driving your car, or simply sitting and looking out the window, become wholly immersed in whatever you're doing. Focus on the experience and nothing else. Pay attention to the sights, sounds, tastes, and smell associated with whatever you're doing. Stay alert.

As you begin to focus on the external stimuli associated with your current surroundings, start to train your focus inward. Pay very close attention to the physical sensations you are experiencing; feel your arms resting on your chair, feel your posterior snug in your seat, notice any slight aches or itches or pains or pleasant sensations on your body. Breathe deeply. Listen intently. Become as intensely, physically conscious as you are capable. Interpret nothing, label nothing. Just observe, and be.

. . .

I SPEND A lot of time thinking about the Big Bang. The majority of the Earth's scientists are confident that that's where it all began; that's how we all got here. It's impossible for the human mind to contemplate a vacuum, but try it with me: picture an infinite void. Imagine a blank canvas that stretches in every which way indefinitely. Now try to picture an enormous galactic BOOM; a thousand paint cans of a thousand different colours hurled at that canvas at the same time. Try your best to wrap your head around the cosmic collision of forces resulting in the genesis of our galaxy, our solar system, our planet, our oceans, our continents, our ecosystems, our species, our countries, our cities, and you.

That BOOM was you, light years ago. Your physical form and consciousness represents the outer reaches of that BOOM realizing itself. The energy of that original collision of forces isn't exhausted; it is you. Your life force represents the impetus of the universe realizing itself.

And it's not just you. It's your mother and father and your friends and everyone you do and don't know and everyone who came before you and who will come after, not to mention every other animate and inanimate object in the cosmos.

When you practice being fully, physically conscious in each and every moment, the universe opens up to you, and you begin to realize your oneness with that bowl you're washing; your unity with the street you're walking; your connection to your partner that goes beyond the emotional, or sexual.

Practicing this type of intense, fully-present consciousness helps us realize our unity with all things, and thus, our sense of isolation from others begins to fade away. You begin to realize that your loneliness is a sham—you don't need someone else to make you feel less lonely because you are already, inherently, one. You aren't really lonely because you are not, and never can be, alone. This isn't some type of new age fluff; it's scientific fact.

Your relationship to the world—to other humans, to other animals, to plants, to inanimate objects, to all things—is one based on mutual dependence. You would not be without the universe, and the universe would not be without you. Because you depend on the external world for life, and life depends on you to carry on living. It is impossible for you to be alone as you are one with all things, as all things are one with, and in, you.

In each moment we make a choice: to be present, or not; to acknowledge our unity, or not. And thus, in each moment we have the ability to choose to be happy, or not.

6. LOVE

TONIGHT I SMOKED a cigarette on the roof and listened to Bob Dylan sing "Visions of Johanna" and missed a certain woman more than I have in a long time. I don't *actually* smoke, you see—I steal cigarettes from my flatmate, and therefore, I am not *officially* a smoker, or so I tell myself. But I appreciated the cigarette and I felt a little nostalgic as I blew smoke into the night sky, looked up at the stars, and missed the girl.

It was strange. I haven't thought about her in quite a while, and what's more, there are new women in my life—good ones. But still, I pictured her warm naked body and one particular afternoon in which I saw her most-vulnerable, least-guarded smile, and I missed her. I missed her body and I missed her voice and I missed taking walks with her, and the fighting, and the bullshit, and the way it felt to get close to her once again.

I don't know where she is or what she's doing tonight, but she's out there, somewhere. Perhaps she's taken to amateur smoking, as I have. Perhaps she's in some other city on some other roof enjoying a Marlboro and missing me, right now.

I loved her, or at least I thought I did for a little while. But she was too young and too guarded to build a life with, and that's ok. Besides, you can't really "build a life" with anyone. In fact, I hate the expression. We make our own way, each of us, we build our own life, and sometimes we have company for a little while, and that's fine. But you can never really "build a life" with someone. If you make the attempt, you spend the rest of your life trying to make two uneven, crooked puzzle pieces fit together, and that's insane.

Still, I miss her every once in a while in odd moments and it catches me off guard. I'm thinking about the last time we listened to *Blonde on Blonde* together. That really was the album where Bob decided to say "Fuck it" and own his strange, theatric, ugly and beautiful voice, and really ham it up. I used to impersonate him in doing so, and it made her laugh.

Right now I miss her, and it's rejuvenating at the same time. Because I'm alive, and this missing reminds me of it. This cigarette tastes better, and I can hear and understand the music in a way I've never been capable of before...

Ain't it just like the night to play
Tricks when you're trying to be so quiet?
We sit here stranded
T   *hough we're all doing our best to deny it*

The girl could be anywhere tonight, but she's not here, not in this strange and wonderful city with me. I hope she's happy. I hope she has a good and strong man to hold her and keep her warm, if that's what she wants. I miss her, but I don't want her here, and I don't want her back. But I'm grateful.

I'm grateful for her helping me understand what it is to feel pain, and how to overcome it. I'm grateful for all of those nights when I missed her as she was laying right beside me. I'm grateful for the nights that came after when I didn't, and she wasn't. I'm grateful for the memory of her skin and smile and laugh and a hundred nights spent wrapped around each other.

I can remember one night so clearly.

She was wearing a white towel wrapped under her arms, and her hair—her wild, wavy blonde mane—hung down well past her shoulders. She had just gotten out of the shower and her skin still felt warm, and smelled like soap. Soft to the touch and olive-white, her skin always smelled and felt so fresh, so inviting.

She walked in from the bathroom and sat down on the bed next to me. I remember tracing the outline of her back and neck with my fingertips, following the trail with soft kisses. She had a small mole in the centre of her back which drove me crazy; another smaller one on her neck which I found even more compelling. She was radiant and fragile, and in that moment, she was all I wanted. Holding her body close was like stepping into a warm bath on a cool night with the window cracked open.

It was late at night and she was sleepy, but I wasn't; I was captivated. Captivated by her curves, her tired smile, her perfectly-unselfconscious beauty. She had deep, dark blue eyes which you could dive into forever, and I made the attempt as she asked:

"Do you love me?"

I smiled.

"Every once in a while."

She smiled back. "No, I mean it. Do you love me?"

"Yes, I do."

"Really?

"Very much."

Her voice turned quiet. "You love me?"

She smiled again, but I could tell she wasn't satisfied. Neither was I.

I grabbed her by the shoulders and kissed her like I meant it, because I did. And in that moment we were united by something that neither of us could understand or explain; there were and are no words that could capture that feeling, and we were both glad because of it. I pushed her into the wall of the bedroom, my hands exploring her thighs and back, and we kissed for what seemed like hours until finally I could take it no longer. I picked her up as we continued to embrace, and together we fell into bed.

We didn't speak another word for the rest of the evening, and it would be several hours before we would submit to a peaceful and well-deserved rest, our bodies naked and warm wrapped around each other in clean, white linen. A cool breeze drifted through my bedroom window, and as I drifted asleep I can recall an unfamiliar understanding of her, and I, and all things.

. . .

THAT NIGHT WAS important to me. I remember it because it was the first time in my life that I really understood and appreciated the elemental speechlessness of love. As I am drawn to write about joy because it seems so indescribable, so too I'm moved to write about love. I love the way love resists my attempts to pin it down with language; I love the way it eludes capture by my intellect. I love the way love plays hard to get.

Love is the most mysterious of any human experience. Love is reckless and bold and quiet and tender; bringer of infinite joy and immense sadness. Love is hazy and confusing and lucid and everything in between. Love is the best lover and friend you've ever had, as well as your most savage tormentor. Above all, love simply is.

Falling in love can consume us. Sometimes it takes precedence over our day-to-day activities so that we become mostly absent in performing them. Instead, our minds wander to outstretched arms, moist and tender kisses, and the smell of her skin… that skin.

Our love would eventually fade. Over time, our love began to doubt itself and wither and struggle for air until it was gone, leaving a dramatic wake in its absence. For a while I marvelled at that wake behind me, straining my eyes as I traced its path fading into the distance, but the reality was that my ship kept moving. I couldn't tell for a while, but it was true.

Because our ships never stop moving. When we fall out of love with someone that energy doesn't simply disappear; instead, it changes form, as water turns to ice, or ice to water. It is moving and growing and changing within us constantly, and though a significant portion of it may be centred on one person for a period of time, there is always more left to give. For love is infinite, and there are no restrictions on how much we can or should love, or how much we have to offer the world. Love grows along with the rest of us; we can never exhaust our love.

I think the real trick is to love so fully, so passionately, so intensely, so that you'll never look back and regret not loving enough, not loving fully. Whether it results in pain, or betrayal somewhere down the line is immaterial because your love needs to get out; I think all of us are wired so that trying to "hold back" or stifle our love results in the worst kinds of disease and misery. So if you're moved to love someone you simply *have* to do it, which isn't the same as letting them walk all over you, or staying in love with someone who doesn't return your love.

It's fine if you find out someone doesn't love you back, or rejects your love, as you can then find someone else who will. I'm of the opinion that we don't really fall in love "with someone;" we simply fall in love, and for a time that love may be centred on one person, and that's fine. We should give ourselves entirely to loving that one person. But I don't believe in soul mates, or finding the "One." Because there are many "Ones."

I think that god is love, and sometimes we recognize that god in someone else. And that's what we fall in love with; a glimpse of the divine in ourself that we see reflected in another. We "fall in love" with our ability *to* love, which is where the real payoff lies; loving for the sake of love itself, rather than loving someone in anticipation of reciprocal love, attention, or affection. Your joy—your party—will thrive when you let love flow freely through you without *any* expectations.

If we feel we're in love with someone, we should love that person rapturously. But, if things don't work out or our hearts long for more, we will, sooner or later, see that same god in someone else. Because we're all god; we're all love, and we can see it in everyone if we look hard enough. And we *must* have the courage and conviction to go on loving because we can't keep it all inside of us for very long.

I don't know much about love, but I know that.

7. DESIRE

LAST NIGHT I met a woman I wanted very badly.

She was half-German and half-English, and despite being a product of two nations not known for their warmth, she exuded it in abundance. Her eyes were the brightest, most expressive shade of green I've ever seen, and she had a toothy, goofy smile which I found endearing. She had wide hips and cream coloured skin, and she didn't take herself too seriously, a quality I routinely seek out in lovers. She had a good sense of humour and a severe, very-German hairstyle, and I thought she was damned fine.

It's been a while since I've responded to a woman like I responded to her, and so I woke up this morning feeling energized. I'm reminded of the power of wanting, and the value of wanting, and how much value desire can bring to our lives, if we take the time to think about it, and respond to it properly.

We can choose to interpret and experience our desire however we want. We can cling to what we want, thirst for it, and let it disrupt our happiness or we can observe it, understand it, and let it inspire and motivate us to greater things. We can get stressed out and angry when we don't get what we want, or we can breathe and learn from our not getting, and get on with our day. We have that power.

I didn't take the half-Anglo-half-Deutsch girl home last night, but that's alright. My wanting of her is gift enough; I don't need her body, not right now. I think I'll see her again and I would like it, but for now I'm enjoying simply wanting.

Most of us associate "anticipation" with "good things to come," but anticipation itself is exciting and rewarding regardless of whether or not we experience those "good things" in the future. Disappointment often follows anticipation, and that's because anticipation is so enlivening. So, often when we get what we want a) it isn't as good as we imagined it would be, and b) the feeling of anticipation was more fun than the payoff. (Anyone who has ever experienced an unsatisfying one night stand will understand what I'm talking about here.)

So how can we respond to the process of anticipation so it can boost, rather than hinder our happiness?

We can watch it.

We can step outside of ourselves and take a look at our desire and think "I want this thing, but I don't need it, and the wanting is fun in and of itself, whether or not I get the thing I want. Because the wanting reminds me of my humanity, and all that I have yet to learn and experience. I am alive and I want and it's wonderful."

The distinction between wanting and needing is crucial here.

As humans, our actual "needs" are scant: food, water, shelter, and perhaps occasional companionship, though there are more than a few monks in the Himalayas who would quarrel with that argument. The point is this: we often think we need more than we actually do.

You don't "need" anyone, and if you think you do you'll spend the rest of your life in constant tension. When you believe you "need" someone your self-worth suffers, your freedom shrivels, and the person you think you need will eventually abandon both you and your neediness. It's no secret that neediness is corrosive to attraction, and is responsible for the demise of many (perhaps most) romantic relationships.

People don't often talk about "attraction" outside of romantic relationships, but it's almost as important for friendships. We are "attracted" to our friends, and want to spend time with them because they provide value to our lives, and we to theirs. I *want* my friends in my life, but I don't "need" them, and I don't think they "need" me either. Any "neediness" in any one of my friendships would turn things sour. Friends are easy to be around; needy people are not.

Why are so many of us repulsed—either consciously or unconsciously—by neediness? What makes neediness so damaging to attraction, communion, intimacy?

I think it's because we want to spend time with people who are aware of their value with or without us. Confidence is sexy, sure, but *value* is even sexier. As non-needy individuals we value their complementary presence in our own lives, and feel moved to give something back. We like it when a friend or lover can stand strong by themselves, and our presence is a mere compliment to their already-rich lives.

Non-needy people demonstrate confidence and strength and a deep knowing of self; our soul or spirit or whatever you want to call it is drawn to know them as they know themselves. I think I speak for most people when I say that I'd rather be shipwrecked on a desert island with a man who knows himself, and his unique strengths and weaknesses, than one who doesn't.

Furthermore, I'm drawn to non-needy people because I'm motivated to grow, learn, and change. I want to surround myself with people who will encourage and support my growth as I encourage and support theirs. When you don't *need* anyone, you only want people around you who will bring value to your life, and inspire creative, boundless growth. Of course, we all "need" to grow as humans as we aspire toward our best potential selves, but when our growth comes from a place of genuine desire and curiosity—not survival—our growth becomes limitless.

Needy people look to others for survival, not growth, and their growth is limited as a result. Needy people look to someone to provide them with X and only X, whereas non-needy people are open to accepting whatever gifts will inspire them to the most growth.

When you think one person can give you what you need you spend the rest of your life chasing a peace that will never come; seeking a resolution that will be forever elusive. It is in our freeing ourselves from neediness, clinginess, and destructive desire that we begin to make peace with ourselves. We then start to seek out the things we instinctively want which encourage and support our growth as healthy, happy, creative beings.

The sad truth is this: most people are needy. Most people look to others for validation, recognition, love, respect. Most people look to others to provide a good time. Most people think they need others to inspire them to party. Most people think they need others to love them before they can love themselves.

What they don't realize is that they have everything they need already. Of course, others have valuable lessons and gifts and value to bring to our lives, but needing or expecting others to fill those gaps will restrict our growth, and bring only pain and disappointment.

Perhaps this neediness is born out of the universal sense of loneliness I described earlier. Perhaps it's low self-esteem. Perhaps it's both. Whatever it is, I think at the core is the individual's unwillingness to take ownership for their own growth, and their own experience of reality.

If you wait for good things to "happen" to you, they never will. If you neglect taking ownership of your personal development, and rely on others to push you, inspire you, and instruct, they will always let you down. If you wait for the party to come to you, it won't.

Freedom is the most sacred, and enlivening aspect of being human. But we can never be truly free if we think we "need" others to complete us, love us, want us, or push us to grow. We have all the tools we need already; we have all the love and motivation we need already.

Freedom can be found in accepting all of the responsibilities that come with our freedom. Real growth comes from taking individual ownership of our growth.

Our freedom, our growth is our responsibility, and no one else's.

8. YOUR GIFT

WHICH TASK BRINGS you the most joy and satisfaction? What do you do that gives you the most pleasure? What is your heart moved to give? What are your hands compelled to produce?

I believe that everyone has a unique gift, but I don't mean it in the bestowed-from-on-high sense of the term "gift." God doesn't enter into what I'm writing about now.

I mean *your* gift. I mean something that is deep within you that you are moved to share with the world. I mean your contribution. I mean that thing that you love doing that makes you feel good in doing, that also makes others feel good in receiving. I also mean that thing that you occasionally hate doing, but know, deep down, you have to do. Some people call it a "fire," but I'm not crazy about the term; sounds too destructive. Your gift is creative. Your gift is your legacy. Your gift is your life force made manifest in the world.

Whether you build a highway or a motorcycle, write a symphony or a recipe, or you simply provide love and kindness to the people around you, your gift is important. Your gift is true; it doesn't lie to you, or anyone else. You know it, deep down. Your gift is selfish and unselfish at the same time. The world needs and wants your gift, as you need and want to give it.

We are now past the halfway mark of this strange little book, so you may very well disagree, but I know writing is my gift. Whether or not the you want to accept it, I know someone will. One person is enough. Because I write as much for me as I do for that lonely reader.

I sit at my computer to do this almost every day, and some days the words flow freely and I feel inspired and happy. Following writing on those days I feel energized like I have just taken a cold swim in the ocean on a clear and sunny afternoon, right after having made passionate love with a beautiful woman. There is an electric spike up my spine and the skies open up to me. I then take a stiff drink, if the writing was good, because I know I've earned the pleasure. For the moment, I feel empty, and complete.

Other days it feels like I am sitting on the toilet constipated after having consumed an entire wheel of cheese; straining, painful, nothing coming out. I struggle and there is a slight, nagging tension behind my eyes when I look for the right words but come up short. I feel a tremendous burden—I know the words are in there, somewhere—but they won't avail themselves of my fingers as I type. I hate this sort of writer's frustration as one might hate a bully in school; I know he's always around the corner, waiting, just waiting to beat me down and convince me of my weakness.

The worst nights are the nights when I didn't even *try* to give my gift, and I know that I could and should have made the effort. The evening's entertainment is always less entertaining, the wine less sweet, and I take little pleasure in my company, however cheerful or interesting. I am uninspiring and often dour, and those around me are cheated of my best qualities.

I know writing is my gift because it's something I have to do, love doing, and occasionally hate doing. My gift is a constant effort; it doesn't come for free. But it is in me and of me and, should I go more than a few days without giving it, I get cranky and awful, and I know it's time to sit down and get to work. And then I feel much better, and my evenings feel much more enjoyable and free.

Your gift may also be writing, or one of a million other possibilities. I can't tell you what it is; I can't see or imagine it. But I want it. I want that thing—that thing that is yours to give—very badly. I want it in all of its its imperfections and oddities and grace and beauty and complication. I want it all. Because I know it's yours, and it's valuable, and it's interesting, and it's different from my gift. If you're moved from your soul to give it, I want it.

And everyone else wants it too; the joyless and the depressed and the deliriously happy all the same. Because the world needs more men and women to give their gifts.

The world needs more men and women who are unapologetic about giving their gifts. And the world needs you to give yours right now.

Because there's no time. There is no tomorrow and there is no next Sunday or next month or next year. There is only now. There will never be a better time to give your gift because there will never be another time to give your gift. Now is it. So give.

Whatever that thing you have to do is, do it. Often. Every day. Even at the expense of your relationship or work commitments or children or whatever. Because everyone in your life will ultimately benefit from your giving, and they want your gift too, even if they don't or won't recognize it.

Your time with them will be more joyful, more interesting, more relaxing if you are giving your gift, in some way, every single day. That tension in the late evening—that "Shit, I should have gotten more done today"—will fade away. Your party, your life, and the lives of everyone you know and love will be far richer as a result of your giving.

Your gift is yours; I can't take it from you. No one can. It's yours, but you *have* to give it. And anyone who tries to convince you otherwise is living in misery as a result of not giving their own gift. So they try to beat you down, or make fun of you, and reject your gift because it reminds them of their own neglect and weakness. But you can't let them get to you—give anyway. They will either gradually warm to your gift, and start to give their own, or they won't, and will live the rest of their lives never knowing real peace.

It's a lot of work, I must emphasize once more. Sometimes it's easy, sometimes it's a little like hell, but you *must* give regardless.

Give your gift with abandon because I want it, and everyone else wants it, and right now is the only time to give.

9. NOBLE SUFFERERS

AS YOU PROGRESS on your party through life, from time to time you might encounter what I call "noble sufferers."

Instead of simply trying to bring you down, or dampen your inclination to party, these people take comfort and solace in their own suffering, convinced that living a meaningful life is incompatible with living a joyous one. They couldn't be more wrong, but don't try to tell them; noble sufferers are convinced that their suffering is justified, worthwhile, and in total accordance with their mission in life, whatever the nature or specifics of that particular mission.

But make no mistake: there is nothing "noble" in their suffering, however much they try to convince themselves (or you). Their suffering is born out of ego and ignorance, and comes at a tremendous cost.

I once met an intelligent and miserable man who was utterly convinced of the intelligence of his misery. When I suggested that a bit of fun and partying might do him some good, he claimed to "not believe" in happiness. I don't remember my response exactly, but I'm certain it involved a blank stare. I'd heard the argument before, but it never ceases to give me pause.

And there was no mistaking the sadness in his eyes. This sadness was no doubt a result of his fetishization of unnecessary suffering. He seemed to think that partying actually *detracted* from his mission in life; certain that living a joyous life was antithetical to living a worthwhile one.

What this ego-driven masochist failed to realize was that his insularity and unwillingness to experience joy prevents the right people from supporting him on his mission; he'll never receive the outside help and perspective his mission requires because he lacks the humility, charisma, and energy of the enlightened partier. And as he proceeds through a joyless existence, refusing to let his love out and let joy in, he will only attract other noble sufferers ignorant of our species' need to party. His mission will remain infeasible and incomplete as a result. All because he thinks he's somehow above getting down, and having a good time.

The more you remain convinced of the seriousness and joylessness of your life's work, the less others are drawn to join in and help. Your ego may try to dissuade you from seeking and accepting help from others, but make no mistake: your mission in life—whatever it is—will suffer without it.

All meaningful professions, purposes, and life missions share a common trait: they are all concerned with the betterment of our planet, and thus, our species. Anyone who claims that partying and joy and happiness is incompatible with their life's mission overlooks one basic and inescapable truth: a certain way to contribute to the betterment of our planet is to experience the most joy of which you are capable, and share that joy with others. This is what enlightened partying is all about, and what the most miserable non-partiers fail to appreciate.

We could spend all day speculating about what drives their fetishization of suffering. We could blame the Protestant work ethic, or capitalism, or the lingering Puritan strain in American society, or any number of other factors. What matters is this: life is a dance, a game, a boundless and limitless party, and when we try to "make sense" of it all, and ignore its inherent playfulness, the quality of our work deteriorates. We lose our creativity, passion, and curiosity; we lose our centre as playful, curious, and unserious beings. Life and living is meant to be fun, and no mission—no matter how seemingly grandiose or serious or solemn—is incompatible with joy.

And if we are unable to experience real joy in performing our labour, pursuing our purpose, and furthering our mission, when can we? If we are seriously committed to some higher calling, or goal, or mission in life, why might we feel unable or unwilling to experience joy in pursuing it? If we are truly in alignment with our soul's highest calling, shouldn't joy flow naturally as a result?

If we take no joy in our mission, perhaps we are not as committed to that mission as we imagine ourselves to be. Perhaps our ego is having a laugh at the expense of our happiness; convincing us of the seriousness and nobility of our mission in order to satiate itself and differentiate itself from the "ignorant," partying masses. Our ego likes to convince itself that it's smarter than everyone else, and fetishizing suffering and repudiating joy is an effective means of accomplishing just that.

Joy is not antithetical to passion or purpose, and partying is not antithetical to hard work. Partying *itself* is often hard work; bringing the most possible light, love, and happiness to the world around you is a full-time job.

Your mission in life will only become more clear, more impactful, and more rewarding when you give yourself permission to experience joy in pursuing it.

Your work should feel like an *opportunity* to party. Your purpose and passion should inspire you to party as you perform your labour.

All of the great philanthropists, humanitarians, and entrepreneurs take joy in their labour. Their lives almost always involve a great deal of difficult work, but their missions are all joyous: joyful because they are aware of the impact they are having on the world, and the happiness they are providing the world through their labour.

Whatever your mission or purpose or calling in life, strive through the world without trying to carry it on your shoulders. Don't use the gravity of your labour as an excuse to not enjoy yourself as you perform it. To borrow a phrase from Alan Watts, in this life it is better to be "not serious, but sincere." Life is a game, and if you choose to not play along and enjoy yourself, you and everyone you care about will lose.

When we die we are not defined by our labour. We are defined by the impact we had on the living.

10. COMPLAINING

MY FRIENDSHIPS ARE starting to change as I grow older. In my younger years, I felt like I exercised more agency over who was, or was not going to be my friend. I feel like I chose who to grow close to. I'm not so sure I choose any more. It's almost like I inherit my friends as part of some pre-ordained plan; God, if you like, somewhere above the clouds having a good laugh.

However they come into my life, I feel a great deal of responsibility for my friends. I want them to be happy. I don't want them to marry that awful woman. I want them to get away from that abusive man. I want them to lighten up. I don't want them to become an alcoholic. I want them to admit that life is really, really good. I want their lives to be filled with peace and joy.

It might reveal (ok, it certainly reveals) a bit of arrogance on my part, but it comes from a good and genuine place, I assure you. Of course I don't always think I know what's best for my friends. I just want them to be happy.

One of my friends has an incredible life, and I do mean incredible. It's painful and frustrating to watch my friend live his life up close because he has no idea how incredible it is; or, at least he usually refuses to acknowledge it. Let's call him Greg.

If there were an Olympics of complaining, Greg would take the gold, silver, and bronze medals in every competition. He's the Usain Bolt of bitching; the Michael Phelps of moaning. Most of us enjoy, or even feel we "need" a good moan every once in a while; Greg takes this to a different stratosphere.

His internet connection is too slow. His drink is too weak. Some business associate screwed him over eight years ago. You looked at him funny. He didn't care for the tone in your voice. You're a disappointment to him as a friend. Everyone in his life is a disappointment to him. It's not him, it's you. You're the self-serious bastard, the whiner, the problem. He's just "being real, man." "Being himself."

The flip side to this character makes itself most apparent when Greg's drinking. When he's sober, he can be insufferable. When he's drunk, he's the best friend you've ever had:

He loves you. He loves life. He wants you, and everyone else, to be happy. No, seriously, *he loves you, man.* He wants to go to Indonesia, the Bahamas, Beirut together. Let's buy matching hats. Next round's on me. Ain't life grand?

But by tomorrow afternoon the Olympic champion is back at it. Everything disappoints, and the complaining starts.

I exaggerate, but you get the point.

Greg makes a decent income, has a kind and considerate boss, and does work that he believes in. He has a wide network of friends and relatives who care for him. He's good looking and intelligent. When he's not complaining, his wife and children adore him. He can disarm you with his laugh, and when properly inebriated, he can be a *hell* of a good time. His party usually needs some alcoholic lubrication to come out, but it's in there. It's in him.

I like Greg. I want his approval, his friendship, his attention in a strange way. The problem is he can often be a miserable prick and sometimes it's tough to be around.

There's the selfish element to it: I want him to lighten up because his energy feels pretty draining a lot of the time. But I mostly want him to lighten up for his sake, because I know there's a better way.

However, I am *not* trying to suggest that I never complain.

As I write this I'm recuperating from a semi-serious injury that will keep me bedridden, celibate, and sober for at least another two weeks. It's not pleasant, I don't mind telling you. I want to go outside. I want to be able to walk from room to room and not hurt. I want a mid-afternoon romp with my girlfriend. And for god's sake I want a gin and tonic, and don't think for a second that I haven't expressed the same to friends and family.

But a funny thing happens to me once I start going down the "woe is me, pity me" route. I start asking myself: what's the point? No really, *what's the point?*

Why do we complain? And what's more, what do we, and the people we complain to, get out of it?

We complain because we seek understanding, company, and pity. Maybe we can blame our mothers. If we're born lucky, our mother's love is infinite. As children, if we fall and scratch our knee Mummy's love becomes overabundant. Words of comfort, hugs, and pats on the head. "Oh poor baby, I bet that hurt didn't it?" Yes, Mummy, yes it did. Keep the unconditional love and affection coming, thanks.

When we get older we keep looking for the same thing in different forms. Instead of hugs and pats we crave sympathetic ears, reassurance, recognition. "Oh, poor baby" becomes "That's too bad" or the ubiquitous (and frequently disingenuous) "Oh, I'm so sorry to hear that." Whether we get delayed at the airport, or fired from our job, sympathy can be nice. We want people to see and relate and really *feel* something for us in our suffering. (Again, it makes us feel less alone.) But do they *really* sympathize with us?

I'm not so sure. And what's more: do we really *need* that sympathy? And do we need to complain to get it?

Of course we don't. And when we complain we bring others down and share a bit of our pain and disappointment with them. This raises the issue of why the hell we *want* to spread our suffering around for others to share, but I won't get into that right now. (We humans are a strange tribe.)

We define ourselves as victims when we complain. When we complain about something we are announcing to the world "Life isn't so great, and I'm a victim of circumstance." We either ignore or reject our power to *do* something about whatever is upsetting us, and our suffering/frustration/dissatisfaction goes on.

It takes a lot of energy to complain; we usually become animated and dramatic in the act of complaining. We really put on a show; a tedious and predictable show, but a show nonetheless. Our voice becomes exasperated, and sometimes we even adapt different characters in trying to illustrate who or what is disappointing us. I'm convinced that most "storytelling" that takes place between friends and family members is actually just theatrical complaining.

Go to a coffeeshop for the sole purpose of eavesdropping. (Bring a book and pretend to read, so as not to arouse suspicion.) Most people around you will be complaining. Groups of two are the worst, sharing the mundane details of minor daily setbacks as if they just arrived home from two tours in Iraq. Their food was late, the traffic was awful, their boss is an idiot, their boyfriend neglects them, etc. etc. If you're anything like me, you will be astounded at how many anecdotes shared between friends roughly equate to this: "Some person in my life is unintelligent/unpleasant/unreasonable, and I am a far more intelligent, reasonable, and all-around better person by comparison." Most of the time they won't come out and *say* that, but the implication is clear.

I do it, you do it, we all do this to a certain extent. But what if we didn't?

What if we channelled all the energy we put into complaining toward actually *doing* something about our problems? Why don't we focus on what we can fix, and ignore what we can't? Why don't we say "OK, this thing happened that I didn't want, but to hell with it—I choose to be happy anyway?"

Because that takes work. That's not easy. The easy way out is to say "Woe is me, the world is a nasty place, you should pity me." Actually choosing to *do* something about it takes a rare and formidable courage, and decisiveness.

This is what's so frustrating about Greg: he has the strength, intelligence, and the means to solve his problems. He can fix the damned internet. Deal with that guy at work. And he can stop asking me to hang out if he doesn't care for my twisted sense of humour. For Christ's sake, man: *do* something, instead of just complaining about it. It's not always easy, but it's easier than you think.

There will be a constant downpour on Greg's party for the rest of his life if he doesn't change. There will always be *that thing* to carp about: the pizza didn't arrive on time, that woman betrayed him, we're out of whiskey, whatever. In the meantime, he'll miss the myriad of gorgeous lights, colour, *people* that surround him, day and night.

I hope you understand by now that I'm writing to myself at the same time as I'm writing to Greg. My own inclination to complain is both ridiculous, and a complete waste of time. There are abundant opportunities for me to mould and break and twist and work and shape my life into anything that I want it to be. So why waste energy on complaining? I *need* that energy to build my ideal life.

Furthermore, everyone around me needs all the energy they can get to build their lives, their parties, into something magical. Why deplete their energy in my juvenile quest for sympathetic ears?

We may delude ourselves into thinking that we just need a "good rant" once in a while to feel better, but this relief is temporary and illusory. Temporary, as any "relief" we experience will soon be succeeded by an additional list of complaints, and illusory because *we never experienced true relief*. When we complain we are saying that we're basically powerless to change our lives, and I refuse to accept that there is any relief to be found in such a cowardly, and pathetic affirmation.

So stop complaining. Make a decision, and *do* something about your problems.

Otherwise, let them go and move on. There are no other options.

11. THE JOY OF OTHERS

"HAVE YOU EVER known real joy?" I turned around in my seat and asked the passenger behind me.

"Uh… what?"

"Have you ever experienced real joy?" I asked, looking him straight in the eye.

I was riding shotgun in a Colombian taxi, turned around in conversation with one of the back passengers, an American tourist in his mid-30's.

Night had fallen on the city of Medellín, and a slight and exhilarating cool had overtaken the city streets. It poured in through my open window, and I was grateful for the relief from the mid-day heat.

We were relocating to another pub on the other side of town with fellow happy travellers looking for a good time. I was feeling energized, a little drunk, and uninhibited enough to interrogate my new friend.

John sported a pasty white complexion, messy brown hair, and a short beard. He had sunken, limp eyes which seemed to wince when I looked into them. He wore a baggy grey shirt and torn black jeans which suggested to me that he didn't care a whole lot about his appearance. I'm not suggesting that he should, but his sense of fashion on a Friday night seemed to make it intentionally clear. I didn't particularly care what he looked like, but I did care about his answer to my question.

"Uh, I don't know…" he replied.

My roommate at the time sitting beside John smiled, familiar with my half-inebriated propensity to inquire new friends about their joy.

"Really?" I insisted.

"Yeah… Actually, no—sitting here talking to you, Zach. Joy!"

John smiled and I smiled back, and we all laughed, and for a moment I felt a little guilty for being a little abrasive with someone I just met. My regret, however, was quickly replaced by sympathy for my new friend, who obviously had never considered my question.

I'm sure that John had experienced some joy in his life—after 35 years, how could he not?—but it was clear to me that he thought my question bizarre, and unserious. I later assured him that my question was absolutely serious, as I believe it one of the most important questions we can ask ourselves as humans. So ask yourself:

When have I experienced joy in my life? Do I experience real joy on a regular basis?

If the answers are anything other than "Often" and "Yes" to those two questions, something needs to change.

You don't need to be as obnoxious as me to question others regarding the same. And I don't ask people these questions to be obnoxious or nosy—I ask because I'm aware of the impact that these types of questions can have on the person being asked. I'm also selfish:

Asking people to reveal the source of their joy causes them to experience joy. Most people who answer questions regarding their greatest pleasures are overtaken with a sincere and obvious glee at the prospect of reliving that joy in order to properly explain it. And what's more— learning about the joy of others encourages us to be open to joyful experiences we may not have appreciated before. In the process, their joy becomes ours, too.

I once asked a man about joy and he told me about wine.

Merle was an Australian backpacker in his mid-60's, with shaggy, long grey hair and a dark tan accrued over many years of outdoor work, and travel in tropical countries. He revealed to me that his greatest joy in life involved sitting on his back porch in the early evening with a glass of merlot, watching the sun fade over the hills behind his property. He loved the smell of the trees wafting in with the night air; crisp, clean, ancient. For as the trees grew and aged, so did the man; he told me he appreciated their scent, and their gentle reminder of the changing nature of all things. As the trees breathed, so too did the wine, and he appreciated the mixed aroma as he uncorked the bottle, and let the wine sit for a few moments before tasting it. As he described the scene to me, his face took on a nostalgic, peaceful air, and his whole body seemed to relax. I could tell that he was already looking forward to the following evening's indulgence, and after talking with him that night, so was I.

The following evening my own merlot tasted better, I took more pleasure in drinking it, and, most importantly, I took the time and effort to appreciate the wine for the miracle it was. Merle opened my senses up to a joy I had never really experienced and, to this day, I believe I take more pleasure in an average bottle of wine than the average person. That was Merle's gift to me.

My father also likes a glass of wine, but he likes the morning more.

Throughout my youth, on any given morning my Dad was the first one to get up in our house, usually rising several hours before me, my mother, or my little sister. For years I marvelled at his discipline for getting up at the ungodly hour of five o'clock, until I really began to understand how much it meant to him. My father really does *love* the early morning. For him it offers a sense of peace, and is an essential time for isolation and reflection before the days' activities begin. He can watch the sunrise and drink his coffee and be totally alone with his thoughts as his brain awakens from sleep and his body comes to life. I can tell that he needs those early hours spent in isolation and reflection in order to make the best possible use of his day.

Unlike my father, I've always loved staying up late at night and sleeping until late in the morning. I still remember how exciting it felt when I reached the age when my mother could no longer impose a strict "bedtime," and I was free to stay up as late as I wanted. It's 11 pm as I write to you now, and I can hardly recall a time when I've written anything of value before 8 or 9. For me, the night feels mysterious and full of possibilities, and I love staying up until the wee hours writing, dancing, laughing with friends, or enjoying the company of a desirable woman. I need late nights on a regular basis, or the days seem too long in anticipation of the night's work and entertainment.

But my father taught me to take joy in the morning, and I now do so on a regular basis. For my Dad, most mornings are joyful, and what an extraordinary and valuable joy that is. How many of us can find significant and consistent joy at 5 AM? My father can, and through describing it, shared that joy with me. I'm still a nighthawk, but on those mornings when I have to get up early, I do my best to appreciate it. It's much easier now because of my father's gift.

Happiness is contagious; joy is contagious. And however much we feel like we know ourselves and what makes us happy, there is always more to learn. Show me a man who has "settled" on his joy—on what he likes, what he doesn't like, and the limits of his growth—and I'll show you misery.

We are born to grow, and change right up until our dying breath. And if you think you know the limits of your joy, you're wrong. It takes a peculiar and gargantuan arrogance to claim that you've exhausted your joy, for no being on Earth is capable of doing so. You can't exhaust your joy because you *are* joy itself.

So question others about their joy, so they can share it with you. In doing so, you will encourage and inflame their bliss as you explore and expand your own.

12. CHASING PLEASURE

YESTERDAY A TALENTED actor and charming human being died with a needle in his arm. Today we all feel cheated. What other work could he have produced? Where would his muse have taken him in the future? The way he died was cheap and sad and frustrating. "For what?" we ask ourselves in vain.

His audience lost a beloved entertainer, but others lost a father, a son, a friend, a lover.

He died chasing pleasure, or running from the pain, I'm not sure which. There is often very little that separates the two.

There is much that distinguishes chasing pleasure from joy, however. Experiencing joy leaves one feeling energized, inspired, and awakened, while chasing pleasure leaves one feeling empty, tired, and unfulfilled. In the case of the actor, and more than a few great talents before him, it can also lead one to exit the party long before their time.

We have all watched a friend, a loved one, or even a hero squander their time, talent, or fortune in the name of chasing pleasure. Perhaps we, too, have wasted days, months, or years seeking a high that would never come, whether through drugs, or sex, or a promotion, or any other temporary thrill. In so doing we waste our party and exhaust our spirit looking for happiness as something external; something "out there" to be found, rather than something within to be cultivated. For happiness is not external, and looking for it in outside experiences will only bring frustration and pain. The moment we discover that we are the arbiters of our own reality is the moment we begin to transform our reality into whatever we choose. And our reality can be joyous, if we choose.

The high you or I or anyone else is looking for won't be found in a needle. Nor will it be found in a bottle, or a naked woman, or skydiving, or travel, or any other external stimuli. It is in you and of you. All you have to do is recognize it, and let it out.

There is a wonderful quote by the Buddha that roughly translates from the original Sanskrit to this:

"When you realize how perfect everything is, you will tilt your head back and laugh at the sky."

When you realize that you have all of the joy and happiness and pleasure in the world at your disposal all day, every day, you too will have a good laugh. And you will have earned it.

Most people never realize this, and spend their lives chasing something outside themselves with the hope that it will make them truly, finally, happy. But it won't.

When I was a younger man I refused to give myself permission to be happy. Whenever I found myself feeling good, I would try to shut it down and think to myself: "Sure, you *think* you're happy now but what about X and Y and Z? What about all the work that's left to be done?"

"What about those last ten pounds that you should lose? You can't be *really* happy… not yet."

"You're several thousands of dollars in debt. Do you think it's going to take care of itself? You don't *deserve* to be happy… not yet."

"What about that project that you started, but never finished. Other people are waiting for it, and you're letting them down. Happy?"

"What about that terrible thing you said two weeks ago? What about that? Still happy?"

As you can tell, I used to have very negative self-talk. There was a miserable bastard in the back of my skull, keeping me down and refusing to acknowledge the light in the world, the good stuff. He had a caustic, childish, annoying voice, always straining to keep my joy in check.

What's worse, I would attempt to satiate my need to experience joy in the moment by building up an imaginary future happiness into something mystical. I would tell myself to wait—just wait—until everything in my life is perfect. Then I'll have a *really* good time, and I can finally be happy.

"Just wait until X, Y, and Z are finished, and you've lost that weight, and finished that project, and paid off that debt," I would think to myself. "Then you're going to be happy. So happy. You can relax, and party all the time, and there will be gorgeous women all around and a mariachi band in your house and you'll have your own yacht and an endless supply of rum and coconuts and..."

You get the picture. It was ridiculous.

As you can probably guess, that imaginary future happiness never came. Because I kept adjusting the finish line to happiness every time I accomplished something. While I worked toward that future happiness, more tasks, responsibilities, pressure, and stress would enter my life. And so I'd come up with a new laundry list of tasks to be completed before I would let myself be happy. Needless to say, the yacht and mariachi band never materialized.

I don't think I'm the only man to submit himself to such torture. As men, we often feel that we must work, and work very hard, before we can party, relax, and experience real joy. We need to grind ourselves into the ground in pursuit of future happiness, and then one day— one glorious day—the hard work will be over and we can finally rest and be happy. Everything we need to do will be finished, and we'll finally reach that finish line.

It's insane.

A few years ago I realized how insane this game was. So, I decided to give it up. I'm very happy as I write to you now, and I have more responsibilities and pressure in my life than ever before. More debt, more responsibilities, more stresses. Not to mention the fact that I've got a hangover that just won't quit, some strange throat infection that makes it difficult to swallow, and a fresh pimple on my forehead the size of a Buick. But I don't care: I'm happy.

The work will get done, my headache will cease, my student loans will get paid, my pimple will recede, and my throat will heal with a bit of tender loving care. I'm happy, and no one and no thing can take that away from me. It's my decision, and it's final.

It took me a while to realize it, but *choosing* happiness, and deciding to *enjoy* the pain and stress and hard work and put my faith in the universe that it will all work out doesn't lead to stasis.

"Happiness" is a dirty word for some, and I can understand why. For some, "choosing to be happy" implies a laissez faire attitude and a lack of ambition; confining oneself to a life of dopey mediocrity.

But these people have it all wrong. Whatever you want to call it—happiness, joy, whatever—it allows the real work to get done. When you choose to be happy, the stress surrounding the work to be done and the pressures and stresses of life start to dissolve, and you can work toward your goals from a place of optimism, and clearheadedness. Gritted teeth and wrinkles don't get good work done—happiness does, because happiness leads to inspiration, and creation follows inspiration.

But some people don't realize this. Some people feel that they are unworthy of happiness altogether, and confined to a life of toil and hardship, convinced that happiness will—and should—never come. Perhaps they are noble sufferers, convinced that their labour is joyless and solemn and serious and has no room for bliss or joy or silliness.

This is one reason why people chase pleasure, and neglect joy.

Chasing pleasure is a cheap and easy escape. We go to the bar after work and drink a pitcher of beer and, for a brief moment, we take ourselves less seriously and laugh and forget the fact that we don't deserve, or cannot experience, happiness. The pleasure is fleeting and hollow, but we don't care. We need to chase it because we only have one or two nights a week before we have to return to our labour, and wait another week to experience a bit more pleasure.

Hundreds of millions of people live like this. Hundreds of millions before them did the same, right up until their dream of future happiness died along with them.

Living like this is wasting time. Living like this is a terrible waste of energy and resources. Living like this comes at the cost of your mental well-being, physical health, and your joy and the joy of everyone you love.

And here's the kicker: the people who profit most off the needless pain, toil, and postponed happiness of others are the most miserable bastards of all. They are the ones who tell you that you need to work harder, suffer intensely, and spend money before you can party. For them, happiness comes with a price tag. They tell you that you won't be happy until you give them your time or money, and they feel like they won't be happy until they take it. A perverse marketplace such as this can only breed more perversion, and so everyone tries to forget the ugly cycle in a fit of drugs, cheap thrills, and empty pleasure on a Friday night; a vicious orgy of hollow consumption every weekend.

But you can't let the bastards get away with it. You can't let them think you'll play their game indefinitely. You can't let them tell you that you can only kick it and get wild on a Friday night if, and only if, you worked your ass off the rest of the week. Or worse—work your ass off for fifty years until you can retire, old and sick and sexless, crippled after half a century of backbreaking labour and empty excess. No, you can't let them get away with it…

When you start checking out of this corrupt state of affairs the bastards start to sweat. And that's good—we want that. Because a) they could stand to use to lose a few pounds anyway, and b) that means we're winning. Joy is winning over unnecessary suffering.

You can love the bastards in spite of their nature. I do (honest). But you can't let them win. Turn away, draw your own conclusions, concoct your own philosophies, but never—ever—let someone else define the limits of your joy.

13. PRESENCE

TOMORROW YOU ARE going to die.

I'm not suggesting that you will die in the commonly understood sense of the word. Tomorrow *might* be your last day on Earth, though it's unlikely. I'm saying you'll die tomorrow because we all die each and every day, an infinite number of times throughout the day, quite literally. You'll die tomorrow just the same as you died in your sleep last night, or as you enjoyed your bowl of Cheerios this morning.

Early in the last century, Western scientists proved what a few Eastern sages discovered centuries prior: that at the same time as we are constantly being born, we are constantly dying.

The cells in your body are being generated, transforming, and dying at such a rapid rate that you are hardly the same person, biologically speaking, that you were five years ago. In truth, you are not the same person you were five *seconds* ago; countless cells have died, and new ones have been generated, since you began reading this paragraph.

Forget about your soul, forget about your ego, forget about the past, forget about the future, forget about whatever you consider your personality: in each moment you are new. In each and every moment you are born again, and at the same time shedding the corpse of your former self. You don't exist—you *never* existed—in the sense you may have once thought you did.

Cells present for your formative years as a child are long gone. Countless cells present for the most important events of your life departed years previously. You die, and not just once, but in each and every moment. This, too, is part of the glory of life: as we are continually growing, transforming living beings, we die at the same time.

As I asked you in previous chapters to move deeply into your own death, start to think about the tiny deaths you experience each and every day, in each and every moment. Life and death are in union within and without you; dancing together, as a man and woman on a ballroom floor, to some timeless, rhythmless, ancient hymn.

The question then becomes: why bother with trying to hold onto your "self?" It isn't there.

Similarly: why try to hold onto a party? It, too, is momentary and in perpetual flux.

Let's talk for a moment about that party.

You are one of several partiers gathered around a living room, drinking, dining, dancing. Everyone is drinking, but just a little; still sober enough for real, deep, meaningful laughs and conversation. Everyone is happy. Everyone is alive. It is miraculous.

So why try to hold onto it?

Why take a photo? Why "check in" with some cheap social media update? Why text an absent friend to let them know about the good time they are missing?

There's a better option: be totally present, and enjoy. That's all.

Drink in this party like it will be the last party of your life, because that's exactly what it is. Soak in your company—revel in your friends' warmth, their conversation, their compassion—because it will never be the same. Stop, and bear witness to your surroundings, from the carpet beneath you, to the ceiling above you, to the empty glasses and bottles of every different colour decorating the kitchen table, take *everything* in.

Because this is it. This is all that exists, though it will be gone in a second. This night will never repeat itself —*you* will never repeat *yourself*—and if you are interested in cultivating the most joy possible for you and your companions, you'd better recognize it. Because you will all die tomorrow, never "remembering" a thing.

Your hangover is irrelevant; the amount of liquor you consumed the night before doesn't matter. You didn't "black out:" you could have spent the evening totally sober, and it wouldn't have made a difference because we don't "remember" things like we imagine we do. As we are born and die constantly, so too do our memories. However, our "memories" are never, ever, as pure as we imagine them to be.

What is a memory? Most people think that a memory is a vivid recollection—a mental documentary—of past events. We assume that our brain records the events of our lives in glorious high definition video, storing it in the hard drive of our brains for safe keeping, and future review.

In fact, our memories are more like impressionist paintings with constantly running, wet ink, than they are like video tapes; a living, breathing, changing and eventually dying animal, as opposed to some static museum piece. Our memories are as alive as we are. That said, they are subject to the same basic principles of life as we are: they are born, and change, and die, over and over and over until our time as mortals is through and we face our final departure.

Any comfort or inspiration you derive from past memories is delusional, as your memories are delusional. Your memories trick you into thinking that life can be lived retroactively, but they lie to you; they are funhouse mirrors, obfuscating and obstructing your vision of whatever reality you once experienced. They are shadows lurking in the night, offering empty intrigue. Your memories are phonies.

So your false "memories" of that party don't matter. Your cheerful recollection offers empty happiness that is ultimately harmful; sedating your need to party now, and encouraging you to make the attempt to live through past glories.

Your memories will die tomorrow. You will die tomorrow.

Your memories are dying in this moment, as are you.

So while you're still at that party, so why not go out in style? Why not honour your life by living as fully, as intensely, as fantastically as you are capable before you lose the opportunity?

You will never get another chance to party like you have the chance right now, in this moment. So when you party, party like you'll die tomorrow, because you will.

CONCLUSION

I KNOW TWO men who were born in separate small towns in Canada during the Great Depression.

Both boys grew up with miserable and cruel fathers. They were each subject to regular beatings, humiliation, and the constant fear that, one day, their father would do real physical harm to their mother. In all of their years their fathers never spoke a kind word to them, and they were each made to feel like they were an embarrassment and disappointment as a son.

They each had younger sisters. They loved their little sisters, protected them, and did their best to be a positive male influence in order to contrast with their fathers. Neither boy wanted his sisters to grow up believing that all men were like Daddy.

When they reached their late teens they each got out from under their father's roof as quickly as possible, and married their high school sweethearts. They each moved to bigger cities several hours away from their childhood homes, and got to work on building careers and families. This is where their paths began to diverge.

One of the men, we'll call him James, began to exhibit his father's meanness and cruelty to his own family when the time came. Furthermore, in private he described everyone at work as an "asshole," and he took little pleasure in his career, despite his impressive achievements. He felt that life seemed nothing but intense and constant struggle, and his anger at his father and himself and God only grew as he advanced in age. He rarely voiced this anger to people outside of his family, and this confused and angered his children. Why are we the only ones who have to listen to his bitterness, they wondered.

He was respected, but not particularly liked at work, and this increased as he rose through the middle ranks of his company. When he retired the party was a rather formal, joyless affair for everyone involved. As he grew into an old man, his pessimism grew so much that he seemed a cauldron of negativity repellent to everyone around him. This inspired his children, grandchildren, former co-workers and friends to pay him only occasional, reluctant visits. The primary victim of his anger and tension was his wife; her nerves grew so bad in old age that her hands developed a constant trembling.

The other man, let's call him Richard, tried to let go of his childhood pain and anger as the years wore on. He was far from a perfect father and husband, but he tried his best and his family loved him for it. He grew out of an angry young man into a well-adjusted, happy and energetic middle-aged man. He treated his wife and children with kindness and respect even when he didn't receive it in turn. He was among the most popular employees in his office as he was promoted to middle management, and when he retired the party hall overflowed with well-wishers intent on seeing Richard off in style.

As Richard grew into an old man his wonder and curiosity never ceased. His grandchildren appreciated this and visited whenever they could, while his old friends and children remarked that it seemed like Richard was "getting better with age;" growing more peaceful, more at rest with himself, and his past, as the years went on. His wife continued to adore him through their fiftieth, and sixtieth wedding anniversaries, and slept soundly beside him every night; knowing, in her bones, that she made the right choice in sharing her life with him, and loving him for all of these years.

Today, the main thing that distinguishes Richard and James is not their families, or careers, or finances, or living circumstances, but their perspectives.

Richard could have grown into a bitter and isolated old man like James. Like James, Richard grew up with a savage brute of a father, endured countless challenges and setbacks throughout his life, and never acquired a vast fortune.

But unlike James, Richard chose to party. Richard chose to rise above the pain and anger that his father caused him, and use it as motivation to grow into a better man. As a result, he became a loving father, friend, and husband. He also inherited the joy that his own father never experienced, and his life was far more peaceful, productive, and rewarding as a result.

This isn't some made-up, feel-good, self-help fable; these men are real. And they've inspired me to think long and hard about which perspectives I want to develop and cultivate as I grow older, and which ones aren't doing me —or the people I love—any good.

Your enjoyment and appreciation of life depends almost entirely on which perspectives you adopt, and which you discard; deciding which perspectives are serving you and those around you, and which are not, and making decisions based on that.

Your ability to party through life mostly depends on how you choose to look at it. And you have the power to look at it however you want.

...

IN THIS BOOK, I've offered you the most important lessons I've learned about experiencing greater joy and happiness in everyday life. I've tried to share with you the practices and perspectives that work for me, and which have allowed me to be a happier, more peaceful person than I've ever been before.

As should be abundantly clear to the reader by now, if it wasn't before picking up this book, I don't have it all figured out. (Not by the longest of long shots.) Were I to re-write *Everyday Joy* in twenty years it may gain a few hundred pages in length, or be reduced to a single sentence, I'm not sure. I think the central component in growing happier and healthier is simply being open to your perspectives changing, naturally, gradually, or perhaps abruptly, and being open to strange ideas, even ones that you may be initially inclined to dismiss as ridiculous (for example, "partying all the time"). One of the main reasons the aforementioned James is so miserable is because, somewhere down the line, he became totally shut down to growth, never questioned or challenged his perspectives, and settled on a limited, myopic definition of self. And so, he suffers, never approaching his true potential, never undoing the shackles of his imagination, and never knowing real joy; real peace.

If nothing else, I hope this book has shown you that achieving happiness isn't as hard as many people make it out to be. It's mainly about being present, being grateful, and making a choice, rather than feeling like you have to suffer for years before it's within your grasp.

But before I leave you, know this: if this book helps you grow into a happier person, some of the people close to you will be upset.

It's a curious thing; how, sometimes, we don't want the people around us to grow too tall, for fear of their vision and ambition outstripping our own. That is to say, if you put the ideas and perspectives in this book into practice, and start growing into a happier person, other people will notice, and it'll probably make some of your friends, and maybe even family members confused, angry, or even hostile. I've seen it firsthand over the past couple of years as I've made some big life changes, and grown much happier in the process, much to the consternation of some people who I once thought wanted the best for me.

But they've offered me a valuable lesson in the process. That is: your growth will be forever stunted if you accept the vision of your potential offered to you by others, and choose to live within the narrow parameters of their expectations. So, regardless of what anyone else says or how they try to make you feel, choose happiness. Choose joy. Live a life in accordance with your deepest truths, frightening though they may sometimes be, and put faith in yourself that you know what you're doing. Because you do.

Enjoy yourself, out there.

NEXT STEPS

IF YOU FOUND this book valuable, there are a couple of ways you can help me out:

For one, I would really appreciate it if you could rate and review *Everyday Joy* on Amazon. Reviews are crucial for a book's success, and you writing one—however brief—would put a very large smile on my face. I don't ask for five stars, just your honest opinion. In fact, even if you *hated* this book, and it inspired venomous rage that kept you up at night and pierced through to your very soul, leave a review anyway. I want to know what you think.

You can also refer the book to a friend who you think may appreciate it, or share a link to it on Facebook, Twitter, etc. Word-of-mouth is still the best kind of advertising.

If you're a Twitterer (Tweetist? Twit?) like me, you can follow me on Twitter at @zfstockill. You can also reach me directly at zachary@zfstockill.com. I read and respond to each and every email I receive.

And please visit my website and join my inner circle at http://www.zfstockill.com/signup. If you do, I'll start sending you my free weekly newsletter, featuring updates on what I'm working on, embarrassing anecdotes from life on the road, and all kinds of unsolicited life advice.

Thanks again for your readership and support. It means a great deal to me.

ABOUT THE AUTHOR

ZACHARY STOCKILL is a bestselling Canadian author, freelance journalist, and educator.

He writes about culture and personal development for publications such as the *Huffington Post, Mic, PopMatters, High Existence*, and many others. He has appeared on HuffPost Live and other programs as a guest contributor.

Zachary has been acknowledged as one of the world's leading authorities on retroactive jealousy. In 2013, he published *Overcoming Retroactive Jealousy: A Guide to Getting Over Your Partner's Past and Finding Peace*, and founded RetroactiveJealousy.com, the most popular site on the internet concerning retroactive jealousy. Zachary is also the host of "Get Over Your Partner's Past Fast," an online course in personal development available via Udemy.

He holds a Bachelor of Arts in History from the University of Ottawa, a Master of Arts in Globalization Studies from McMaster University, and a Master of Arts in History from the University of British Columbia. In addition to his studies in Canada, Zachary has also studied at several institutions in India, and spent extensive time performing research, and enjoying life throughout the Indian subcontinent.

His hobbies include making music, travel, and writing about himself in the third person. Zachary is a guitarist, singer-songwriter, drummer, and budding ukulelist. His favourite Beatles record is the "White Album," which should tell you just about anything else you may need or want to know.

Visit his website at http://www.zfstockill.com.

Printed in Great Britain
by Amazon